AN INTRODUCTION TO
THE SOCIOLOGY OF EDUCATION

AN INTRODUCTION TO THE SOCIOLOGY OF EDUCATION

by

KARL MANNHEIM

and

W. A. C. STEWART

LONDON

ROUTLEDGE & KEGAN PAUL

NEW YORK: THE HUMANITIES PRESS

First published in 1962
by Routledge & Kegan Paul Limited
Broadway House, 68–74 Carter Lane
London, E.C.4

Reprinted and first published
as a Routledge Paperback 1970

Printed in Great Britain
by Compton Printing Ltd.
London and Aylesbury

ISBN 0 7100 3416 4 (c)
ISBN 0 7100 6897 2 (p)

Contents

v

PART V: CONCLUSION

Introduction

THIS is the last of the posthumous volumes of Karl Mannheim's work and now that five earlier volumes have
appeared since his death in 1947, we can put them
together with the books published in his lifetime and realize
the grand scale on which he worked. Any book on education
would refer only to a part of Mannheim's preoccupations,
although, characteristically as we shall see, education in his
hands develops a pretty grand scale of its own. So it is
appropriate that this book should appear last in the canon.

A second apt reason for this book coming at the end is that,
although education was throughout his writings a dominant
theme, the material on which this book is based is probably
more incomplete and more fragmentary than the sources on
which all other volumes were based. The main reasons for this
are not far to seek. Since 1940 Mannheim had lectured on a
part-time basis at the University of London Institute of
Education, while continuing his main work as a sociologist at
the London School of Economics. In 1946 he was appointed to
a Chair of Education at the Institute of Education, which he
held for only a year. Thus, while he had always been engaged
in and by the issues of education, and for a few years had read,
as his enormous bibliographies testify, with characteristic
industry and eclecticism in what the Americans call 'the
area', the concentration of thought in his post as Professor of
Education was tragically short. In 1946 he had a field of study
rich in possibilities and virtually unexplored in this country
where his discernment and ability for synthesis would have
found scope.

There is a didactic element in Mannheim's later writing

which is implicit in the whole theme of the Third Way and planning for freedom. He saw more and more clearly that 'real planning consists in co-ordination of institutions, education, valuations and psychology'. For him education was a means of influencing ways of living and thinking and was also an expression of the nation's institutional, social and philosophic values. Mrs. Floud, in a most valuable essay on Mannheim* points out that his message or policy begins and ends with a concern for the transformation of modern man, and this is borne out by a passage taken from the last chapter of this book:

'(In the study of the sociological foundations of education) we are in search of something which should never be lost sight of in our research. We want to understand our time, the predicament of this age and what healthy education could contribute to a regeneration of society and man. In this quest for orientation sociology is a tool and we shall use it in a two-fold sense as a special theory of education and as a new approach to its history.'†

He maintains that there are no limits which can be laid down for this by philosophic discussion, but that these will appear as a result of sociological research. However, most of his educational thinking seems to proceed from the application of general principles and not from field work as an inquirer, but this is true of his grand manner sociology as a whole. An American writer‡ goes so far as to say that Mannheim is not a sociologist, but a political theorist whose work deals more with the humanistic foundations of education than with the behavioural sciences, for it is quite inadequate from the point of view of experimental sociology. It is true that in one voice Mannheim says that by sociological inquiry we must find out what are the facts, and in another what ought to be done in order to produce certain results. Education is an activity peculiarly suited to this kind of treatment, for by definition it is deliberate, purposeful and concerned in some way with aims. Yet it also is especially open to experimentation, fact-finding and assessment.

* In *The Function of Teaching* (edited by A. V. Judges). London. Faber and Faber, 1959. pp. 40–66.

† See below, p. 160.

‡ Paul Nyberg: *The Educational Implications of Karl Mannheim's Sociology.* Unpublished thesis for Ed.D. of Harvard University, 1957.

INTRODUCTION

Without in any way wishing to let loose the hungry hunters who range about seeking what they may devour in the search for 'a valid methodology' or 'a means of verification in the social sciences', I would point out that education is concerned with people, learning, institutions, knowledge, evaluation. Experimental sociology lets the light strike on it all from one angle, psychology from another, philosophy and history from yet others. Education is a marvellously rich quarry from which to hew academic nuggets, and some of the deposits are so complex that the various prospectors do not yet know how to examine them. At the risk of being cloven by a sociological spade or a psychological pick, I would say that if ever any study was inter-disciplinary it is education. It is liable to serious distortion if any particular scholar gets his magnifying glass on just a part of it.

Mannheim was asking questions which led more and more to synthetic rather than to exclusive and analytic types of thinking. Let us for a moment look at some of these. Individuals live in groups. In what senses has each a unique personality and how is this formed? The human being who knows and what he knows and the act of knowing present problems which have concerned philosophers, psychologists and sociologists since the beginning of time. In what ways is a person free, or limited, or conditioned in his knowing? If we try to place these questions within a particular historical context we have to face the problems of social structure, social control and social change, as well as more generalized philosophic issues. Such themes as these lead to synthetic rather than to exclusive types of thinking.

Mrs. Floud says that Mannheim looked not at flux but at balance at the heart of things. She considers this to raise the classical problems of social statics—the relations of the individual to society, the reconciliation of freedom and organization. Mannheim's attempt to provide a planned, dynamic equilibrium has been commonly and understandably misconstrued. The machinery for equilibrium is not worked out, once for all; the balance itself is not struck, and there's an end of the matter. He says that we now know and can know more of the causes of friction, dislocation, breakdown in societies and we must learn to cultivate 'a rational mastery of the

ix

human situation'. This is not social statics, it is social dynamics, it is both balance and flux at the heart of things.

This distinction between statics and dynamics is not a return to the familiar verbal springboards from which to try to take off in some novel fashion. I want to make clear that Mannheim was not specific about change in the way that Marx was, because he did not undertake to analyse historical processes in detail, although he was more specific after 1933 than before. Instead, he tried to indicate the key points at which the diagnosis would have to be made each time—economics, property, law, consensus, the nature and influence of élites, individual and group values, communities and 'massification', the meaning of freedom, education. What the *content* of the changes would be, how they should be brought about in any situation, he did not often try to specify in any detail. Here again we are dealing with a grand scale sociologist. The method of approach was there and this was the dynamic element in so far as it was applied, and the continual equilibrium in society was the ever-changing goal which has always to be approximated.

After 1933 when he came to England he turned his attention from general theorizing to the specific crisis of the Europe of the thirties and pursued there his perennial quest for continuity, not at any price, but with democratic purposes in mind. His particular concern after 1933 was a natural consequence of his earlier quest for a sociology of knowledge and a sociology of culture, and to that extent represents a reasonable continuity. Obviously it leads on from his own experience both in Hungary and in Germany. How hauntingly a sentence at the beginning of *Man and Society* read at the time, and still reads 25 years later.

'To the Western countries the collapse of liberalism and democracy and the adoption of a totalitarian system seem to be passing symptoms of a crisis which is confined to a few nations, while those who live within the danger zone experience this transition as a change in the very structure of modern society.'

The socially unattached intelligentsia can no longer afford to speak with detachment. Life or death for democracy hangs on accurate and comprehensive social analysis, some of it for critical immediate purposes, some of it to define and articulate what a democratic society entails. If Mannheim added little to his diagnosis of the crisis after 1933, he began seriously to consider the next stage—what could be done about the crisis. This, he admitted, was a change of interest, for he says at the beginning of *Man and Society* that the German version* was written in the conviction that the democratic system had run its course because the Weimar Republic had revealed the help-lessness of the old *laissez-faire* order to deal with modern mass society either politically or culturally, but when he got to England he found a much more deeply rooted liberal demo-cracy, which tempted him, as he says, to an optimism that would make him forget that we were all living on the edge of crisis. While some academic sociologists might regard this as a disappointing decline into special pleading under the guise of the application of a still sketchy 'method', Mannheim himself undoubtedly regarded it as part of his academic pilgrimage, the application of principle to an apocalyptically urgent situation.

Mannheim saw man as a biological, social and psychological organism, influenced by, 'conditioned' to the stimuli about him, moving towards a greater and greater comprehension of his own impulses and mastery of the social keyboard. How men learn and what they learn can be charted. What they *ought* to learn is not only a psychological or sociological matter and Mannheim declared himself for democracy like any liberal politician. But for him the problem still remained: *how* do men learn even what they ought to learn? How far should people of different levels of insight in a society comprehend its co-herence? In any case this coherence rests not only upon the co-existence of institutions like family, government, authority, exchange, labour, law, organized education, but also upon control and knowledge of indoctrination, the understanding of mental and emotional process. More centrally still, the coher-ence rests upon the sense of individuality, the self-awareness of the person and his perception of the relatedness of his ideas and of things.

---

* The book appeared in a much shorter German form, *Mensch und Gesellschaft im Zeitalter des Umbaus*, published in Holland by Sijthoff in Leyden in 1935 after Mannheim had left Germany. The English version was published in 1940, by Kegan Paul, Trench, Trubner & Co. Ltd., London.

II

THESE are some of the guide lines within which Mannheim's ideas on education were worked out and in this book we are able to take these formulations farther than has hitherto been possible. The argument in Part I concerns both terminology and viewpoint. He believed that those who have studied education have accumulated a great deal of reliable knowledge which is too little known, particularly in the fields of history, psychology and sociology—he was even prepared to talk of a scientific pedagogy and the inter-disciplinary outlook necessary for it. In England we have a number of ideas and value judgments tangled together in terms like training, instruction, teaching, education, and in unravelling these Mannheim pointed to the need to differentiate between narrower and broader definitions of education:

'We should, therefore, distinguish between formal, institutionalized aspects of education such as are to be found in the schools and the broader, more generalized notion of social education which arises from the influence of the educative society where we are educating through using community influences . . . Here we are dealing with both the school in society and the school and society. That is to say that education has to be considered as one and indivisible in which formal schooling, vitally important as it is, must in all parts be related to other factors in society.'*

To use community influences meant, for Mannheim, paying regard to the ideas and ideals which have established themselves from generation to generation in Western European history, and he indicated some of the main educational ideals from Greece, Rome, Palestine, medieval Europe and elsewhere which have persisted.

I said earlier in this Introduction that Mannheim concerned himself with exploring the meaning of the phrase 'personality of the individual' and the senses in which men may be said to be free or limited or conditioned in their knowing. In this book this theme appears several times, the first in Chapter V dealing with the contrast of the individualist and the collectivist in their views on education. The individuality, the self, says Mannheim,

* See below, pp. 19-20.

ought not to be viewed only in philosophical terms, but should be seen also as an aspect of developmental psychology according to which higher learning, personal experience, conscience develop out of an elaboration of the simpler processes of infantile conditioning, and from the interaction between an organism and its physical and social environment. So we pass in the total argument of the book to Part II, where psychological matters are more closely considered.

To what extent do we possess innate tendencies and what do we mean by instincts as distinct from habits? Mannheim gave hints in a number of his other books that he was interested in psychoanalysis, although his references were often interesting animadversions rather than developed argument. The bibliographies he left behind him and some of the references in this chapter show that in his last years he was reading widely in the works on learning theory and trying to discover his own answers from the behaviourists, the gestaltists, the social psychologists, the psychoanalysts and from dynamic psychology in general. The whole of Part II of this book extends what he has previously written on psychological subjects and gives promise of what might have followed as he strengthened his grasp of these ideas and built them into his sociological synthesis. In Chapter VI he states that there is as yet no one authoritative psychology and so he repeats the characteristic method of Chapter V (and earlier books like *Ideology and Utopia** and *Man and Society*) by showing the polarities of the behaviourists and the dynamic psychologists within which, as time passes, an increasingly coherent account might be expected.

He follows this discussion of the flexibility of human nature and the whole matter of social conditioning with a more detailed treatment of human learning, what are its characteristics, how it may be helped and how it may be hindered. For him discussion of learning moves quickly from the structure of the process to its content, from concept formation to the notion of role-taking and to the multiplicity of roles expected of anyone in our society, out of which what G. H. Mead (a name important to Mannheim which we shall meet again) called 'the role of the generalized other' emerges. But Mannheim returns to the 'laws' of learning as Thorndike and Hull

* Mannheim, Karl: *Ideology and Utopia*. London. Kegan Paul, 1936.

have formulated them and relates role-taking to the 'laws' of exercise and effect especially as these may be observed in the classroom. In the chapter on inhibition in learning he sums this up:

'Important as associationist theory is in understanding the learning process and in attempting to offer a descriptive system, it seems only of limited use in educational psychology because the relationship between the teacher and his pupils involves the personality of each . . . Besides this personal relationship there are the roles to be played by both pupil and teacher which give to and maintain in the relationship a certain structure. I would maintain that dynamic psychology can give a much fuller account of what takes place than can associationist psychology.'*

If learning may be said to be the main theme of Part II, the nature and growth of personality is the theme of Part III. The self is not given at birth or any other time but emerges out of our social experience and here Mannheim explores in greater detail what G. H. Mead meant by the 'I', the continuing self, and the 'me' which is the more or less integrated set of attitudes and ideas which we have built together as our conscious experience from which we choose roles to represent our own ideas of ourselves (which may very often be what we know the community has come to expect of us). While different aspects of 'me' depend upon my social and cultural training, my memory and experience, the 'I' is the self as actor or initiator, the agent of change. Moreno (another social psychologist who was important to Mannheim) explores the same kind of analytic problem, speaking of 'the content self' and 'the act self'.

Mannheim's purpose in calling these (and other) students of personality development into the discussion is to counter what he calls the passive and manipulative aspects of the notion of adjustment with a theory of man the initiator, a creature who is in a real sense autonomous. However, as he says, in our day-to-day behaviour and in our educational practice we can emphasize either conditioning and control or spontaneity and creativeness, and in fact we tend to move from one to the other, although in schools we are prone to rely more upon one or another form of competition or compulsion than upon spon-

* See below, p. 83.

taneity and the pupils' initiative. In society at large also we move between these two poles—creativeness, responsibility, the qualities of the original and the originator; and conformity, subservience, the qualities that bring people together in co-operative groups.

In Part IV we come to the sociological factors although the border territory of social psychology is crossed more than once. What are the responsibilities of the home and the school? Are they always complementary or do the functions of school and family change as children grow older and their stake in society changes?

'The crux of the whole matter is whether we can manage to convince ourselves and future generations that there is a difference between education and passing the time and that we must use all possible agencies to enrich education not only during a period of what we become used to as compulsory education but through the voluntary acceptance of the compulsive quality of education during the whole of life.'*

The last two chapters of Part IV come close to the problems of the teacher or the intending teacher. The first applies sociological principles to the classroom and the teacher's role in the school. The second (*Sociology for the Educator and the Sociology of Education*) is in some sense a summary of what the rest of the book is about presented for the intending teacher and pointed up with this in mind.

The Conclusion (Part V) analyses the whole educational enterprise, and declares without equivocation that our purpose in studying education is to relate it to the aims of an epoch and to build up a reliable sociological theory which we can use in improving the society in which we live.

III

THERE were few relatively complete manuscripts on which any section of this book could be based. Many, many fragments and notes, a very small number of complete lectures with the usual

* See p. 133.

pause and accent markings, sheets of bibliographies, schemes for lecture courses, diagrams for ideas, characteristically bold and handsome doodlings—these constituted the materials from which the book has been constructed. Because I have had to be arbitrary in selection and to be freer in adapting and composing the material than an editor should be, I have coupled my name with Mannheim's as a co-author. While it is true that I have been more than an editor, it is clear that the basic ideas in the book are Karl Mannheim's.

I was a friend and student of Mannheim, and his widow, the late Dr. Julia Mannheim, gave me his education manuscripts to work through for publication. This responsibility I was glad to accept and it was rewarding to enter again his intellectual world although he was no longer able to elucidate or defend what he had written. It was, however, also an exasperating responsibility, from two main causes. First, the fragmentariness of the records, voluminous as they also were. Second, for various reasons, one of which was that Dr. Erös and I edited an earlier book in this posthumous series,* this volume on education is appearing 14 or 15 years after Mannheim's death and my sense of guilt is correspondingly great. This delayed publication does less than justice to the urgency and relevance of his ideas as they appeared in the years after the war. As the psychological sections of this book show, his ideas were being developed and modified all the time, and had he lived (he would only have been in his late sixties now) we could reasonably have expected new concentrations of interest and insight.

This book is, as it says, *An Introduction*. It is not massive, it is in places familiar, it is characteristic in its range of reference and method of attack, it lacks political depth. But it is a reminder of a change in the way of thinking about education in this country which had its origins in many places before and during the war and Karl Mannheim was one of the most important contributors to this transformation. Mrs. Floud concludes the essay already mentioned with words which I am happy to acknowledge and to be allowed to borrow:

* Mannheim, Karl: *Systematic Sociology*. Edited by J. S. Erös and W. A. C. Stewart. London. Routledge & Kegan Paul, 1957. This book was based on more complete records which Julia Mannheim had also committed to my charge.

'. . . It is fair to say that the attraction of his mind and personality had us all in his power. As a Professor of Education his success was astonishing and his death in 1947, at the age of 54, only twelve months after his appointment in 1946, deprived London of a formidable teacher at the height of his powers.'

W.A.C.S.

Keele,
1962.

Acknowledgements

The notes and bibliographies for this volume were prepared by my friend and colleague Dr. John Erös and I am glad to acknowledge his help and advice. We have included almost entirely books and references which Mannheim had listed (sometimes when they were not yet published in this present series but the manuscripts of which he had approved). Very occasionally reference has been made to a book which appeared after his death, but only where it is unmistakably relevant.

The typing and preparation of this manuscript has been in the hands of Mrs. Doreen Brookes and I am grateful to her for her patience and thoroughness.

PART ONE

THEORETICAL MATTERS

I

General Introduction

IN studying education we try to create scope for reflection; and, secondly, to establish the study of education as a coherent body of facts and principles so that the work done in schools and elsewhere should be built upon foundations which are as nearly scientific as possible.

There are some who are still sceptical about both these purposes, considering that reflection in education is scarcely a serious endeavour, and that the principles are no more than amiable discussion of disconnected topics. However, I belong to those who believe that philosophic reflection is even more necessary in our age than ever in the past and that education is becoming not only one of our most important efforts, but that in studying it we have accumulated a great deal of reliable knowledge which is too little known. I think that the time is ripe for us to draw together these findings, but it would be as well to look more closely at what I have called reflection and to indicate the concept of education and pedagogy which I have in mind.

Whenever a man lifts himself above a specific endeavour and reflects upon it from a different viewpoint he displays an attitude of mind which need not be clearly linked up with systematic logic and metaphysics nor with any other traditional philosophic discipline, but which is related to that kind of thinking. In our everyday approach to things, we necessarily take them for granted and use techniques with which we are familiar, struggling for purposes which we seldom analyse thoroughly. For example, in preparing to teach, one might study a subject and absorb considerable knowledge of it, one might examine the methods of teaching it to children of different ages and, to give some context to the part one intends to play as a teacher, one might study educational administration and institutions, maybe even on a comparative basis. Most of this we would do first of all in a largely factual and non-reflective fashion, taking the inherited aims of education, the inherited techniques of teaching and the established methods of keeping order and preserving discipline, for granted. However, when we reflect upon these matters, we raise questions which reach out beyond our routine activities and habits of thought. We move to a higher vantage point from which we can see the whole situation and not isolated facts. Some of the questions have been asked many times by philosophers and practically-minded men. Consider the following: What is education? What is education for? What are the special tasks and potentialities of education in the situation of the present day? We examine the facts in relation to each other, we trace them where possible to cause and effect, and we evaluate them in terms of performance. John Dewey expressed this as an aspect of culture when he wrote 'Culture . . . is a capacity for expanding in range and accuracy one's perception of meaning.'[1]

The study of education combines and co-ordinates the results of various more or less homogeneous subjects in order to find the answers to the questions which it raises. We have recently been forced to realize that the composite studies are in many ways at least as important as those which are more homogeneous. Consider, for example, the emergence of biochemistry, criminology, geophysics and economics as inter-disciplinary studies. What then are the disciplines which have to be co-ordinated in order to be able to answer the many problems raised by education?

In the past and for many teachers in the present, the emphasis in teaching and learning has been upon knowing your subject. For the rest a 'common-sense' knowledge of what a child is like will enable a man, cultivated by his learning, to teach successfully, which is to say, to teach so that his pupils may learn. However, the more society has grown and its complexity has increased the more we have realized that unimaginative and routine teaching helps to create many misfits, and we have become greatly aware of the fact that the implications of teaching Johnny Latin are more intricate than we ever expected them to be. It is now something of a truism to say that authoritarian methods of keeping order and punishing are more likely to make than to reform criminals. Martin Luther some four centuries ago said: 'It is a miserable thing that on account of severe punishment children learn to dislike their parents or pupils their teachers. Many a clumsy disciplinarian completely ruins children of good disposition and excellent ability.'[2]

Besides admitting that knowing your subject well and having a certain accumulated common-sense experience of children is not enough for effective teaching, it is worth while remembering the simple fact that children spend only a sixth of their lives at school and less than a half of that sixth in school. Hence we ought not to ignore or underestimate the effect of out-of-school life. We ought in fact to enlarge our perspective of what education is.

In 1945 some disquieting statistics were published by the War Department of the United States. Twenty-eight out of every 1,000 recently educated young men were rejected by the army because they were too badly trained to pass even the simplest literary test and were too badly grounded to receive army education: be it noted that these were not registered as educationally subnormal while at school. Or again, in 1939 the Regents' Board of New York State (where expenditure per student is the highest in the United States) published a generally depressing report stating that secondary school children were weak in the knowledge of their own community, ignorant of the history of the United States, ready to think in catchwords and slogans, unaware of the operation of democratic principles, and noticeably reluctant to think of their civic responsibilities. Six out of seven of the children whose cases were considered said that they would refuse a position of responsibility if it entailed personal discomfort. The Regents' Board went on to state that once out of school most boys and girls seemed to read almost solely for recreation, chiefly poor quality fiction magazines and the more sensational newspapers. There have been many similar reports in this country with which we are familiar.

We received a great shock during the war when evacuation

showed us in what physical and mental destitution many children lived. Surveys like *Our Town* or *Youth Service in an English County* or any of the numerous books published since 1940 on such subjects have shown the nature of the physical and cultural conditions endured by many families, particularly those living in large cities. The social services and legislation promoting the punishment of neglectful parents have indicated that the State through these agencies is concerned to try to maintain some kind of standard.

On an international as well as an educational plane, we have been forced to realize that the old social order is in a state of disorganization and so are the people who have lived under it. Services undertaken by the United Nations Organization, by U.N.E.S.C.O., and by the World Health Organization, tend to corroborate that about half the population is living at, or below, a bare subsistence level, and here again what to do, how to have the financial means to do it and in what manner to present the changes, show that some notion of what ought to be is present in the minds of those who are working for material and cultural change at the international level. That this kind of thinking involves educational planning of all kinds does not need to be stressed.

Besides the information that has recently been presented both in this country, in the western world in general, and throughout the countries concerned in the international organizations, we have had in the last twenty years the most conspicuous example of the disorganization of standards and the prostitution of educational ideas. In Germany, the emergence of the Nazi type of character revealed that the educational efforts of a highly educated nation were in vain, and indeed that it was possible to operate the education system to promote the character which is generally condemned elsewhere. In fact, while everybody admits that perhaps the most pressing international problem is that of poverty in the midst of plenty, we have to add that we can have barbarism in the midst of educational plenty. It is not enough to provide educational opportunities, it is equally important that we should understand what kind of effects these educational opportunities are having.

It would appear, then, that at home, as we discovered dramatically during the Second World War and as is known in

6

the daily experiences of many teachers and social workers, educational organization has not only to care for the *élite* but has to improve the conditions of those who are living on a sub-cultural level. In fact, the primitives are not only to be found in some distant countries, but are here among us.

New methods of social surveying applied to education have made a number of important facts accessible. It is now apparent that the distribution of opportunity under the pre-1944 educational system was very uneven and that even when secondary education was possible, it has often been ineffective in its results. In March 1937, of the 560,000 between ten and eleven years of age in public and elementary schools only 80,000 passed on to a secondary school and of these, about 2,500 were likely to reach the universities. In other words, of every 1,000 elementary children, 143 or 14 per cent. reach the secondary stage and less than 0·5 per cent. reach the universities.[3] However, in the United States, the attendance at secondary schools during the first forty years of this century has increased from 10 per cent. to 70 per cent. of the population aged 14 to 18, and there have been similar large increases in university and college attendance. In fact, in some states of the United States, 95 per cent. of those between 14 and 18 have some period of secondary education. Lest it should be thought that the United States has always maintained this high level of provision of secondary education, it should be stated that before 1890 attendance at high school and college was confined to less than 5 per cent. of the population. Therefore, within a period of 50 years, the proportion of young people having some kind of secondary education has multiplied ten-fold, and the number of these going on to college or university education is now three times as many as it was at the beginning of the century. Nevertheless, the United States War Department published during the war the statistics already mentioned referring to faulty training and general illiteracy.

Despite increased facilities for higher education in Britain and the United States, there is much evidence on both sides of the Atlantic to show that the teaching is not proportionately more effective since this vast increase of provision. In some ways this is scarcely surprising since in an earlier time we were educating those who by means of one selection or another were usually

7

above the minimum literacy level, at any rate at the secondary school. With the insistence upon educational provision for all on the basis of democratic principle, we have undertaken to educate the total population and, of necessity, a certain proportion of this population is believed to be of a low level of ability. For all kinds of practical, political and ideal reasons the educational system since 1944 has been re-organized and its total effect upon our society will increasingly be felt during the next thirty or forty years.

When all these matters are taken into account, however, it has to be admitted that our routine technique of teaching is plainly not as efficient as it should be. This is partly because we have only recently given systematic attention to the problems of educating and learning, and partly because our educational aims are inarticulate, not to say confused. The Nazis and the Soviets knew what they could expect from education and we have been very vague about what we really want to achieve by education. One of our valuable but ambiguous principles has been that we must appear to be as varied as possible in our educational system and practice, and that we must not 'indoctrinate'. We are rightly critical of and hostile to what Hitler achieved because his purposes were evil, but we have at least his example to show that a great deal can be done in influencing people through educational practice and organization.

It will already be clear that the study of education must concern itself with a clarification both of what education is and what it aims at being. The definition of what education is involves an analysis of techniques and the definition of aims is concerned with an assessment of values which help to decide, among other things, what methods should be used. Thus, in mentioning the difference between a discussion of educational methods and educational aims I wish also to emphasize the interconnection of both.

When we say that we intend to teach a set of ideas to children we are at once faced with the problem of sorting out these ideas with some precision and our reasons for presenting them. Secondly, we are also faced with deciding the means by which we shall present the ideas. And thirdly, we have to consider what effect both the method of presenting the ideas and the

8

ideas themselves may have. Is educating to mean that we inculcate or indoctrinate firmly and definitely or does it involve guidance only? Perhaps it may be one or the other at different times. Have we in mind the desired shape into which we hope the organism will grow, or is our emphasis upon the growth itself, in whatever way the pupil may choose within the limits of society?

Many teachers are aware of the tension between the amount of information and ideas which should be made explicit and the other effect of the relationship between persons which has a direct and indirect result on the degree of and attitude to knowledge absorbed. Even behind this issue of method there is the major question mark of what can be achieved at all. What can human beings learn to do? How far can human nature be moulded by educational influences? What are the limitations of the contribution of the teacher? What is the significance of the educational atmosphere? These I suggest are all questions which will have a bearing upon practice.

Let us turn for a moment to consider what education is for. Is our aim to educate independent personalities with no particular attention given to the social situation in which they find themselves? Or perhaps the aim may be to educate for adjustment, which some people may consider as a healthy interconnection between adaptable, developing individuals and a changing and developing society. If we accept that this notion of social adjustment is central in human education have we in mind that we should aim at some recognizable type of development while also attempting to grow beyond this type? Many who have read the works of W. E. Hocking or Sir Fred Clarke will remember the importance which they attached to this last point.[4] Even if we accept the importance of society, for which kind of society do we educate? Here we should try to clarify the focal points of advance and deterioration in education for change in a democratic society.

Any student of education has to be concerned with psychology, for in this study he informs himself about the degree of plasticity of human nature. Sociology is also related to the study of education because it deals with the working of society in general and of modern society in particular. It is most important to recognize the kind of influence which a society has

9

upon its members through its institutions and the situations which they create. It is clear that there has been a tremendous advance in the last fifty years in understanding the physical and mental development of persons, but there has been a much less noticeable increase in the understanding of their social development. Education, as it takes place in schools or other institutions, is mainly a social business. It is a dynamic process which is based upon the plasticity of human nature and which aims at a selection of social and personal experiences for concentrated presentation. When we talk about the study of education we tend to think that it should concern itself only with classroom techniques, but this is not so. The classroom and the subjects taught in it are vitally important, of course, but we are concerned in addition with learning, as each person undertakes it, and with all the educational influences which go to form the environment to which each person responds.

Thus philosophic reflection, psychology and sociology are the fundamental studies which together furnish a body of knowledge which is bound to deepen an understanding of, and broaden an outlook upon, education as a whole. Sir John Adams presented a part of this idea when he said 'Education has for its aim to modify the nature of the educand, and not merely to supply a certain amount of knowledge . . . The whole process of education may be said to be one in which the educand becomes gradually transformed into his own educator.'[5]

I would suggest that here Adams has presented to us some of the fundamental value judgments and psychological notions as they relate to education. What is missing is its relation to sociology. In addition to what he has said, we must bear in mind that education has to prepare members of a society to conform on the one hand and, if it is a democratic society, to have the opportunity and scope for individuality on the other. Therefore, we must pay attention to what the society wants of its members as, for example, respect for the law, participation in election of government, a relatively general acceptance of conventions, and a more or less clear understanding of economic motivation. To the comprehension of social institutions and their obvious effects, we must add a recognition that these institutions have latent influences. As an instance of this, it is true that if we raise the compulsory school leaving age to 16, this will offer more opportunity for sound school preparation which may, or may not be directly educational in character; but it is also true that raising the age to 16 will mean that we increase the period of economic dependence of adolescence, and this is the kind of thing I mean when I refer to latent influences.

In studying education, then, we must give attention to sociology because it represents contexts within which psychological and philosophical interpretations may be expressed.

II

Training, Instruction, Teaching and Education

I WANT to draw a distinction between various terms that are commonly used in relation to education. I refer to four—training, instruction, teaching and education.

Training

This word which we often meet in educational discussion has a certain clear connotation and carries with it also often a number of derogatory implications. First of all it can refer to the actual drill or practice which a person may undertake to prepare him for an improved performance, the training which an athlete or an apprentice may undergo, the reference being to the preparation itself whether it be running or gymnastics or the repetition of supervised practice with tools or some other such. However, the additional element which differentiates repetition of this kind from practice is that it is done in the framework of some sort of programme and that there is in the minds of the person supervising the work a goal to the attainment of which each of the steps is part of the preparation. You need to have repetition, improvement and purpose for the word 'training' to have meaning. It may be that the goal to be aimed at exists in the mind of the instructor or that in the case of someone training himself, the same person is both the instructor and the apprentice according to the way in which he looks at his own programme. The trainee may also become his own trainer.

This word has often been mischievous in educational discussions. It is associated with the tricks of the trade, with dependent attitudes and with a limited understanding of the purposes of any activity. Added to which it is directed towards some realizable goal which may be achieved, the limits of the endeavour being relatively clear from the start. It has to do with technique and it is for this kind of reason that 'training' has often helped to confuse some of the principal issues in education. It is significant, for example, that we speak of 'teacher training' and 'training colleges'. At the universities in England for some years the official title for the department of education was 'The University Training Department'. The official title now is 'The University Department of Education'. The training colleges, however, still have this word associated with them. In intellectual activity it is a mark of esteem that you have something more or less independent and individual to say. Training places emphasis upon a man's dependence, upon being taught by others, upon learning within the framework of a known programme.

In the early part of the 19th century in Scotland David Stow elaborated a programme of preparation for teaching and founded what he specifically termed 'the training system', and in this practical work in classrooms played a large part.[1] The Normal School was the accompaniment of this training system —the school from which the norms or standards of practical teaching could be obtained. We are told in Proverbs that if we train a child in the way he should go, when he is old he will not depart from it. This emphasis upon laying down and establishing ways of acting, a routine, a procedure, a solution to all eventualities on the basis of practice, represents on the one hand a necessary part of anyone's mastery of a subject, of a trade, but on the other, in the case of relationships to ideas or to people, it may be too rigid to be creditable.

Here, then, we have a word 'training' which is legitimate in that it defines the skills and practices which have to be understood and mastered but which does not include the equally important principle of independence, the necessity to improvise with all the overtones of judgment, intelligence and freedom which this suggests. It is interesting to notice that training is probably linked with vocational preparation, and education is linked with liberal preparation. Technical education is often thought of as representing the training tradition but technology may give more room for the liberal tradition. In the minds of many people both these words cannot be compared with the use of the word 'liberal' itself. This is part of the inheritance of a humanist emphasis in culture stemming from a pre-industrial age and strengthened by the official approval of an educational system.

Instruction

This word represents the passing on of information. The emphasis here is upon what is communicated and its importance and not upon either the instructor or the pupil. This is another of the words which represent part of the educational process but which very often produce confusion in discussion. We can see this sort of difficulty arising in such a sentence as 'children should profit from the instruction of their elders'. The emphasis in instruction is upon the factual material which is being presented by an instructor. The implication is that the material is clearly understood by the instructor, has been ordered for presentation by him and is presented to the pupil. What happens then is no part of the field of reference of the term instruction. Perhaps it could be summed up by saying that this term represents a state of affairs something like the following 'here is material which has been sorted out to be presented to you. You should absorb it—take it or leave it.'

Teaching

There is a two-fold difference between instruction and teaching which is not easy to disentangle. First the emphasis in teaching is upon a relationship between people, the teacher and his pupils. Secondly there is an implication of the necessity for follow-up so that the teacher may be assured that what he has presented has, in fact, been understood and learned. It is quite true that teaching, like training and like instruction rests to some extent upon certain methods, techniques, tricks of the trade. However, in addition teaching presupposes an interest in the learning process of the pupils and the interaction of the minds of teacher and taught. It is to be expected that the emphasis in this interchange will be now upon the teacher, what he has to say and how he says it, now upon the learner, his growth in understanding and his mental initiative in grasping and transforming what is being presented to him.

The word 'teaching' has also other references arising from historical associations. For example, in England the term 'teacher' has to be differentiated from 'schoolmaster'. This is partly to do with the fact that a schoolmaster in the last hundred years in particular is someone who has had associations with the independent schools or at any rate the grammar schools. He has been a university man, whereas the teacher has been associated with a training college. The word schoolmistress, for various reasons of association, is very often thought to be slightly less advantageous in relation to schoolteacher than the word schoolmaster. There are many shades of semantic distinction which could be followed through here as a by-product of our social history and class structure, but we must resist examining these further. It is sufficient at this stage to have indicated that while the words 'teaching' and 'teacher' have certain associations with the relationship between people and the learning process involved, the shadings of repute can be very subtle and fluctuating.

Education

It is now commonly held that this word derives from *educare* which refers to the bringing-up of children physically and mentally. It is a word of such wide reference that at times it is, of necessity, vague. For example, we read that it is concerned with all the qualities which are acquired through individual instruction and social training, which further the happiness, efficiency and capacity for social service of the person educated. Adams points out that education has for its aim not merely to supply a certain amount of knowledge but also to modify the nature of the pupil. It is noticeable that in the history of the development of the institution of school we have been moving steadily away from the narrower concept of school instruction, of training in specific knowledge or techniques, towards the notion of the school and other agencies as part of an educative society. This is to be detected in the shift and enrichment of the meaning of the word 'education' itself.

It would be wise at this stage to distinguish between the

narrower and wider senses in which this term is used. Wilhelm Dilthey speaks of education as the planful activity of grown-ups to shape the mind of the younger generation, and Adams takes this farther in his examination of the bi-polar process mentioned above.[2] Here one personality acts upon another in order to modify the development of the other. That is to say, that the process is not only conscious but deliberate, for the educator has the clearly realized intention of shaping and modifying the development of the pupil (Adams uses the term 'educand' which, because of its unfamiliarity, we will, for the moment, discard). There are two means by which the development of the pupil is to be modified, first by the presentation of certain kinds of knowledge in its various forms, selected and ordered by the educator in his wisdom, and second through the direct and indirect relationship of the two personalities. It is of the greatest importance psychologically to recognize that only at a relatively late stage, and not always then, can a pupil separate out the ideas which are being presented to him from his response to the personality of the teacher who is presenting them. However, it is probably true to say that the pupil in the later forms of the secondary school, and certainly at the university level, is expected to be able to make this vital distinction. Indeed, we have the curious and inverted view characteristic of some university opinion, and particularly at the older universities, that it is almost an advantage to have mastered your knowledge despite the teaching which you had to undergo.

Dilthey[3] and Adams have this in common, that they see in education the influence of person upon person in which the older generation wishes to prepare the younger generation in terms of idea, knowledge and attitudes. In the foreground of this activity stands the school as an institution in which there is concentrated the purpose of presenting knowledge deliberately and on the basis of a consciously planned programme. Only relatively recently, with the entry of psychological considerations, has the importance of emotional factors in learning and indeed the educational significance of the emotions at large been thought to be important.

This may lead us now to consider the broader concept of education. One of the classical statements of this wider and necessarily vaguer view of education is contained in J. S. Mill's address as Rector of St. Andrews University, Mill said,

'Whatever we do for ourselves and whatever is done for us by others for the express purpose of bringing us somewhat nearer to the perfection of nature (education) does more: in its largest acceptation it comprehends even the indirect effects produced on character and on human faculties by things of which the direct purposes are different, by forms of government, by the industrial arts, by modes of social life: nay, even by physical facts not dependent on human will, by climate, soil and local position.'[4]

There is, in these sentences, a more direct admission of something which has been implicit in the apparently narrower concepts of education mentioned earlier. This is the assumption that education represents the organization of forces and influences which are to lead to a higher standard of behaviour and values—Mill speaks of the effects produced on character. While Adams in the instances referred to has only considered modifying the nature of the pupil, he goes on to indicate that this modification, if it is to be educational in any sense, has to have an effect not only on the increase of knowledge in its intellectual connotation, but also in the application of that knowledge in terms of choice and will.

Education can only arise out of a social situation. Robinson Crusoe could teach himself to adapt to the needs of survival but the heritage of his training and experience as a member of society before he was wrecked on his island gave him resources which he developed with admirable ingenuity and good sense. If the need for education arises out of people living together, one of its aims has to be to enable them to live together more successfully in the widest sense of these terms. Where societies or communities develop, normal ways of organizing their life develop, too, and these the sociologist calls the institutions of a society. Institutions come about from the clash and interplay of individual interests and when they have come into existence they in their turn help to define the area of acceptable conflict and harmony, that is to say they make their contribution to the development of the social and individual aspects of character, where character represents how a man behaves and what his motivation is to behave in that way. Education, then, is

17

dynamic on both sides in that it deals with adaptable development of individuals and equally with a changing and developing society.

How then may we sum up the main features of this broader definition of education? The influence which one person has upon another is only one form which the educative process may take. It is true that this influence may be most complex, subtle and lasting—one has only to consider the importance which is now attached to infantile experience as a factor in the form taken by adult personality to see one very significant aspect of this influence. Or again, the lasting effect made upon us and our standards of judgment through having met and worked with a sympathetic and cultured teacher. Yet, when all this is said, there are other forms of the educative process which have to be taken into account. While we know that the school is only one among the educational environments in which a child grows up (the family being prior and essentially more important) we have now to take more cognisance of the fact that in the school not only the teacher is important but also the nature of the organization to be found there, the kind of discipline which prevails and the environment in which it is set.

III

The Broader Definition of Education

THE main educative agent is the community, the group of people in which the child lives and the objects which these people have created, their relationships, their culture and their connections with a still larger society beyond. Out of such a notion grows the idea of education in adapting to the demands made by the society of which one is a part and implicit within this concept is the recognition of deliberate and generalized influences generated by that society. Sir Fred Clarke uses the phrase 'an educative society' and by this is meant, first, the educative influence of a society, second, the education which may be obtained through membership of a society, and third, education which is related to a society.[1]

As we belong to differing groups whether it be the family, the school, the village, the neighbourhood, the city, the nation, we are educated by and on behalf of standards and ideas prevailing within that community. Forms of democratic government, the profit motive, music, the press, the appearance of public buildings, fabrics, the assumption of the work-leisure dichotomy, the kind of relationship expected between parents and children, the kinds of food and drink and ways in which they are prepared, conventions and social manners—these are examples of the way in which we are educated on behalf of and by the community. If a child is taught to be silent when parents talk or is compelled to wash his hands before meals or to try to talk with a certain kind of accent or choice of language, the mother is conveying to him from the start what are the acceptable ways of behaving, is interpreting the community and how he should respond to it.

We should, therefore, distinguish between formal, institutionalized aspects of education such as are to be found in the

19

schools, and the broader more generalized notion of social education which arises from the influence of the educative society where we are educating through using community influences. We can no longer think in terms of compartments. Here we are dealing with both the school in society, and the school and society. That is to say that education has to be considered as one and indivisible in which formal schooling, vitally important as it is, must in all parts be related to other factors in society.

How have we come to broaden our concept of education in this way? I think there are three main reasons. The spread of democracy, the greater mastery of the social environment, and the importance of the community as well as the home as an educational agency. Let us look more closely at each of these.

The spread of democracy

The obvious dilemma of a democracy is the urge to spread responsibility and reward more evenly over the community, while on the other hand recognizing that not everyone is equally gifted or effective. This shows up clearly and sharply in educational practice. Accepting for the moment without dispute the necessity for universal compulsory education between certain ages, the question of what shall be done during this period arises. In a feudal organization there is a different degree of reward and responsibility accorded to the varying groups. This is not to say that there is not also a general sense of cohesion and loyalty to the system as a whole, but a noble is not to be thought of as requiring the same training as a serf. The liberal education which is important for the free citizen of fifth-century Athens and its transmuted form which was thought appropriate for the aristocrat and would-be aristocrat of seventeenth-century England, differ very considerably from the elementary schooling which was thought proper for the nineteenth-century child of a millworker. Not only were the curricula different but where these curricula were to lead to was also different.

As the rights of man came to be a political principle and as political power was distributed very widely with the expansion of the suffrage, the educational provision in England was called into question. This is obviously a many-sided issue and not only caused by the extension of political democracy. It has to do also with the development of England as an industrial power in the nineteenth century and with the recognition of schooling as an important factor in developing this new urban way of life. It is a truism to say that the elementary school system of the nineteenth century was not primarily intended to have any cultural value but was predominantly and unmistakably utilitarian. When the means of giving this kind of education together with moral and religious principles had been provided, the increase in knowledge and political experience, acting together with the conscience and principle of enlightened men, introduced a new factor. This was the desire of the mass of the people to receive a genuine education as distinct from a vocational training, an education which would enable them to understand something of the world in which they lived and to develop their own imaginings and creativeness, to learn how to read and at the same time to make cultural use of this instrument.

The spread of the ideal of liberal education was bound to transform what was taught and the whole conception of how it should be taught. However, there are two further matters to bear in mind here. What is taught in certain types of schools over a period of centuries has grown out of the social and cultural position of a relatively small and influential group who, as Veblen[2] suggests, have achieved the refinement of culture which they have partly because they are a leisured class depending upon the labours of the majority. This is likely to be the culture of a minority and represents the structure of ideas through which, in part, they express themselves and familiarity with which marks those who have it. In times of social fluidity those who wish to move up the social scale may covet this minority culture and seek it for themselves or their children. Since it is the instrument of a minority, the problem of deciding what may be acceptable to the majority is a difficult one. Should it be a modified form of the refinement of the cultured aristocrats? Will it be possible to spread this cultured heritage more widely without transforming and debasing it? This is the perennial problem of transition from feudalism to democracy expressed in educational terms and it has often been described as the process of levelling up or levelling down.

The same principle applies whether the model is the aristocratic order, the bourgeoisie or the experts.

Another important factor to be borne in mind at this point concerns the introduction of all the technical influences of an industrial civilization to which people must become adapted and which, therefore, directly and indirectly is the concern of education but which is so very different from the type of humanistic culture referred to above as characteristic of the cultivated aristocrat.

What has happened in the spread of education throughout our society is that some of the ideas which were characteristic of education in an earlier order have been carried forward into the new, more democratic order, and as yet an education appropriate for the mass of the people is not sufficiently clear. The new concept of general education is not exactly the old notion of 'culture', and not exactly the ideal of the Christian gentleman with which we are familiar through the tradition of the independent schools; nor yet does it represent the pattern of the gentleman and the scholar though it has affinities with all these ideals. It is something more democratic and something more realistic because it has to define its content in relation to the part the educational institutions have to play in a modern community. This would suggest that there is a kind of basic mental equipment which every enlightened citizen in a democracy should possess, and it is this basic equipment which is extremely difficult to work out. Even more difficult are the forms of differentiation which should be available to each person within that democratic tradition just because he is an individual with his own interests and aptitudes and because he belongs to a group of people and a cultural background which may suggest to him certain minority interests which ought to be part of his educational training.

Education in a democratic state has to guard against the notion that it should be substantially the same for everyone. Natural endowment limits the degree of understanding which different people can be expected to display and the standard of education, therefore, which is appropriate to them. The variety of career available to anybody living in a democratic society is such that many different interests can be served within an educational system as well as a basic educational training provided.

The wrong type of democratic education will tend to transform everything into terms of vocational training and adjustment to an industrial order. It will be so concerned to bring about a compatibility with the contemporary that its sense of heritage, of history and tradition, will be cut at the root. One of the enduring values in the humanist tradition is that this sense of a continuity of human history is preserved and it is important that in any new educational trends the human importance of the knowledge which is presented in the curricula should be paramount. William James[3] went as far as to say that the 'humanistic value of any subject is dependent not upon its content but upon the way it is taught'. This is a statement of the gravest importance in any discussion about an increase of scientific training because of the need to supply scientists and technologists. The schools, it is true, must have a primary concern for the width of the curricula. It is for them to ensure that every child is introduced to what may be done with words, with mathematical symbols, with materials, with scientific concepts, with historical and geographical knowledge, with some concern for values and the human conscience. But when all this is said it is important to go farther and remember that it is possible to teach humane values through the study of science, provided that it is taught with this as one of its aims. Significantly, when we study history, in school, or at the university we think of political history, economic history, social history. Only recently have we come to see that the history of science, the development of inventions is in itself a part of history because it influences the way and speed of life which is possible, it helps to bring about economic and social crises, it helps to change the interpretation of the universe.

Greater mastery of the environment

We broaden our concept of education as we master more and more of our environment. One apparent form of this is the extension of the social services. Here we have tried to combine our concern for persons with our application of an increase in knowledge. We have brought together political and philosophic principle on the one hand and psychological and sociological knowledge on the other. There have been many criticisms of the extension of such services on the grounds of impersonality, of the possibility of interference with individual freedom, of the tendency to sap a sense of responsibility, and so on. While all these criticisms may in some part be justified, the opposite point must also be made—the extension of these services has meant that we have become much more members one of another in the sense that the concerns of far more people are now widely known and we give our approval to a communal responsibility.

Further examples of this kind of concern with the needs of all members of society can be seen in the foundation of child guidance clinics, in the development of settlements and youth clubs, in vocational guidance and the recognition that counselling is likely to help youngsters in choosing work in which they can be both successful and happy. All these institutions and others besides exemplify our attempt to have greater mastery of the environment by shaping the environment itself. This is likely to have consequences of great magnitude for everybody living in a society of this kind.

Besides the establishment of educational services like these, we are now able to communicate with one another far more effectively than has ever been the case before. We can reduce spatial separation by using broadcasting, films, television, and so in this way ideas can be much more widely disseminated and we can come in upon the lives of more people at many points. The importance of some kind of public policy in relation to these great media needs no emphasis. A nation gets the instruction and entertainment it seems to want, is prepared to pay for, and allows to be presented by those who now have made work in radio, in films or on television a career. Because of the power and importance of these media, their relationship to an articulated educational policy, not only for those in schools but for adults, cannot be over-estimated.

To consider another aspect of our interest in our surroundings, let us look at the attempts to plan towns, to influence the spatial layout of our daily life as it is affected by housing, building and the amenities which go with them. It is true that we are only at the beginning of thinking in terms of town and neighbourhood planning and we have a number of dismal examples of thoughtless building development. But when that is said, we have also an awareness now of the need to think on a massive scale of the living conditions of those who will keep the industries going, and when we think of them we have inevitably to think of all the needs of a family in the present day. One of the outstanding needs is schooling and architectural thinking that goes with wise provision for children growing up in schools. It is true to say that some of the most interesting and exciting experiments in building have been carried out in schools in this country since the end of the second World War.

The importance of the community

All the tendencies that have been mentioned stress the point that we are now aware that we educate not only in and through schools but also through the resources of the community. The school must take vitality and relevance from the life of the society in which it is set and it must regard itself as doing work which is unique in that it teaches children that it is reasonable and necessary for them to run counter to some of the currents that they feel in the society round about them. In the past we have not been sufficiently aware of the existence and effect of social education and this is inevitable in a society at the phase of *laisser-faire* development.

A democratic outlook shows itself in the care of citizens for those who deviate from the norm or average of the society. It is very difficult to define what this norm or average is in every particular, although it can be seen very clearly in the case of the handicapped, the blind, the deaf, the educationally sub-normal, the delinquent, and our educational system is now committed to educate children according to their age, ability and aptitude.

This underlines the necessity for offering a variety of educational provision. We are likely to have a period of emphasis upon equality and the need for similarity of provision. But equality of opportunity if it exists alongside education according to age, ability and aptitude must lead to a differentiated educational system rather than greater conformity. Obviously, there are limits within which these principles must operate but it is important to realize that a democratic education which is available to everybody does not mean identical education for everyone. There are some educational thinkers who say that the philosophic and political ideas implicit in this belief have so far only expressed themselves in favour of the handicapped, and while they express no desire to reduce any of the special provision made for handicapped children (indeed, their whole emphasis would be to increase it as much as is necessary) they point out that we make much less obvious provision for those of great intellectual gifts and that the equalizing tendency in democratic education may have narrowed the degrees of difference between one end of the intellectual spectrum and the other to a dangerous extent.

Democracy in its advanced phase is not only sensitive to individual differences according to ability and aptitude but also to differences according to age, social background and previous life history. We now find that a different educational approach is wanted, and different teaching techniques have to be used, if we are dealing with boys and girls, with young children and with adolescents, with grown-ups in adult education, who are engaged voluntarily and part-time as compared with other adults who are engaged in full-time education. There are differences of curricula, teaching method, discipline and control and degree of guidance and supervision.

Or again we find now that while there are many factors in common between the sort of education which is suitable for children living in cities and those living in the country, there are other aspects of work which are different and specific to the environment. It is likely to be much more important for children living in rural communities that they should know something of agriculture than for town children who in their turn might know much more about industrial development and its history. Obviously the kind of local history which is appropriate to the town and the country is bound to be very different and the methods pursued may often be different too.

In addition to the relationship between education and the social environment we find that the valuation of persons affects what is done in the name of education. It is a commonplace of education that we desire not only to sharpen intellectual understanding but also to give place to the emotions in educational practice. There are two main sources from which this trend has developed. The first is the Christian influence on education where from the start the interpretation of the work of teaching has been allied with the notion of the ultimate destiny of man and preparation through childhood for this supra-temporal end. Baudouin[4] suggests that one of the most important contributions of Christianity to human knowledge was this proclamation of the limits of reason and intelligence and the deeper and more significant affirmation of belief in the soul. It is quite true that in the English educational tradition religious influences in the life of the school have often led to repressive control of behaviour and the inculcation of a sense of sin and inadequacy. Even this, in its way, is a belief in something which goes beyond the development of the intelligence through training. In the last century and in the last fifty years in particular the creative possibilities of the emotions have been widely accepted in educational circles, though not so widely exploited in our grammar schools and universities. In our infant schools the case is very different.

In the nineteenth century the ideal of education as it took place in the public schools has been stated in words of Dr. Arnold as the education of a Christian gentleman. Here, besides education of the intellect through the instruments of Latin and Greek there was the discipline of the Christian teacher, attendance at chapel and membership of a community which was devoted to Christian ideals, and these engaged the emotions and the will as much as the intellect and the mind.

The other source from which a contribution came to the educating of the emotions was psychoanalysis. From the beginning there has been present in the new-born infant a desire for satisfaction for and expression of the emotions. There have been what Freud calls the sexual and aggressive tendencies. Any adequate education has, therefore, to take into account the existence of these tendencies and their striving for expression. This, the psychoanalysts would claim, means a deepening of the significance of the term education. Not only is it concerned with the training of the intellect and with the evidence offered by examinations or other forms of intellectual achievement. In addition they would claim we are deepening our interpretation of the personality who is being educated. If we accept that in some ways the conscious mind, of which the intellect is an expression, has arisen out of and is vitally related to the unconscious mind, then we should recognize that education is concerned with the unconscious attitudes of each pupil. Likewise, when we demand standards of pupils we are expecting them to respond and co-operate both at the conscious ego level, and at the super-ego level from which the urge to conform to the standards arises, in ways which are to a large extent unconscious. Super-ego might be said to represent the hinterland of which the ego is the coastline that may be seen from the seaward side.[5]

It is clear to all of us that teachers are engaged in teaching a subject and maintaining standards in relation to that teaching. However, they are also engaged as personalities with the personalities of the pupils whom they are teaching. It is no longer sufficient to isolate the teacher as an instructor bearing authority, who is a channel for a subject bearing authority. If there has been a re-valuation of the pupil as a person, the same is true of the teacher who is gradually being turned from an authoritative and possibly authoritarian instructor into a guide who relies upon the initiative of the learner and recognizes that for good intellectual learning a prior condition is emotional respect between teacher and pupil. In other words we are paying attention to the children whom we are teaching and the ways in which they learn. We want the learning to be not only an acquisition of knowledge which can be recalled and analysed but also part of a personality whose range goes far beyond what he knows with his intellect. What we teach grapples on to the previous experience and present needs of the pupil. If we are dealing with adults obviously their experience and needs are widely different from those of a child. We recognize this in the forms of teaching which are to be found in, say, the early years of the secondary school and the undergraduate years of the university.

We are still discussing the broad definition of education and the importance of the community in this broader conception. We have to recognize that the contributions to educational thinking of Christianity and psychoanalysis have in part influenced and in part been influenced by the political context. The transitions from teacher-centred to subject-centred to child-centred are paralleled in democratic changes which were taking place in the political organization of the country at the same time. Democratic procedures in politics have led to democratic procedures in education. This can be seen both in relation to the rights of men to have educational opportunities with the corresponding compulsion on children to attend schools. So one of the political consequences of democratic rights is democratic compulsion. But in addition to this large-scale consequence, we may detect also the spirit of democratic behaviour and the equalitarian tendencies in the internal organization of many schools. It might be said that the child-centred curriculum is a homologue of the right of the consumer to have some say in what he has to purchase. Or again it might be said that the tendency now to frown upon a teacher who adopts an authoritarian rôle is parallel to notions of equality to be found elsewhere in our social and political system.

It is quite true that there have been educational experiments over the last two or three hundred years—for example Thomas Day and his attempt to put into practice the educational principles of Rousseau; or the brothers Hill and their experimental school at Hazelwood; or the new community in Lanarkshire where Robert Owen tried to set up an industrial and cultural commonwealth. While there have been isolated instances of this kind, it is significant that an organized body of opinion in education made itself felt only at the beginning of this century, and may be called loosely the Progressive Movement.[6] It would not have been possible for an organized movement of this kind to have gained much publicity until there was a highly organized school system against which, in many particulars, the new movement felt it should rebel. The New Education Fellowship begins as a loose federation of unorthodox schools at the beginning of this century. The emphasis in many of these schools and in the movement as a whole was upon 'self-realization of the individual'.[7] Such a slogan obviously needs qualification and definition if any exact meaning is to attach to it but for our purposes it is sufficient if we point out that the ideal of the Christian gentleman at the public school presupposed a conformity to certain patterns and norms of behaviour and procedure and this had become stylized in terms of prefect systems, 'fagging', the predominance of classical learning and an emphasis upon the importance of games. A great deal has been written on the principle of conformity as the basis of the so-called public school type. Against this the progressive schools sought to present a greater opportunity for difference of interest, difference of taste, difference of activity, so there was usually very little emphasis placed upon the prefects, there was no 'fagging' system, new subjects were introduced into the curriculum which were neglected at the public schools—subjects like art, music, crafts, estate work out of doors, and in place of the single emphasis on games as the only acceptable physical activity the progressive schools presented a more flexible pattern whereby those who had no particular preference for the main game played in school could play other games or could, in many cases, choose to work on the estate or could take exercise in their own way. If this kind of change may be summed up in a phrase, it could be said that the public schools represented an imposed conformity and the progressive schools had as their goal an imposed diversity.

To try to do justice to these polarities would demand an historical treatment of the development of the two points of view. What can be seen is that as time has passed each view has modified the other. The public schools have come under criticism among other things for the ideal of conformity, for the absence of a sufficiently flexible curriculum and they have in many cases modified their procedures. The progressive schools have come under criticism for an excessive individualism which, it is suggested, led to a social irresponsibility and they in their turn have in many cases modified the extremism of their position. We are now no longer certain that there is an established method of teaching and that there is a quantum of learning which is all that can be judged of what a pupil has taken from his time at school. We now know that the method has to vary according to the subjects, according to the learning situations, according to the kind of students and according to the depth of understanding which has to be achieved. In addition to all this we have of recent years had to face the fact that the curriculum itself needs to be re-assessed and re-mobilized as times change and subject barriers dissolve.

We have observed how biology has entered into school curricula in the last thirty years and is now an accepted part of teaching, but the content of biology is changing all the time. Chemistry has been in school curricula for longer and so, too, has physics, but again the content of each of these subjects has changed dramatically over the last twenty-five years, and what Ralph Linton called the cultural lag is apparent in the curricula being taught in schools in these and other subjects at the present time. To take a further example, in our school curricula there never has been any representation of the social sciences except for geography, a study which has entered into the majority of schools within the last sixty or seventy years. Within the last half century the study of psychology, of economics and of sociology has developed very fast at the university but not at the school level and we are now seeing an increased concern for the teaching of social studies which is itself an amalgam of separate subjects under the general heading of the social sciences but in addition it embraces the social aspects of science and technology and of communication. In fact we are seeing here in the school curriculum a slow infiltration of relevant material which is establishing its respectability at the university level before it is being translated into subjects acceptable at school. It is because of the transitional nature of the social sciences at the universities that geography finds itself in a position of confusion, or perhaps it would be truer to say in a position of profusion. Here is a subject which looks towards the sciences in its relationship with geology and biology, towards the arts in its relationship to history and towards the social sciences in its relationship to economics, politics and sociology.

We are now far less able to depend upon authority, be it the authority of the teacher, the book, the classic, the work of art, the great idea. The exclusiveness of book learning which was a mark of educational sophistication based upon the abilities to read, to comprehend, to memorize and to recite—this exclusiveness is being challenged. In another way it is being accentuated in that now through the recording of research and through the differentiation of specialists there is an increasing tendency to detailed mastery in great depth of a narrow subject range and a reduced emphasis upon the necessity for wide though necessarily less profound knowledge. However, in these days students are much more participators in the direction of their own learning, they are much more encouraged to discover for themselves through the use of libraries, laboratories, attendance at conferences and participation in committees and other forms of self-government. It is obvious that this changed concept of learning will have its effect not only on the curriculum but also on the examination system. We may expect that the standards and tests on which we measure progress will

4

change and that increasingly careful records of the individuals and the work they do will supply more data for educational and vocational guidance than has been the case in the past. We can see this operating in selection for secondary education in schools. There has been over a period of years a growing criticism of reliance upon test results and a desire to have an increasingly detailed picture of the psychological development of each child and so we find the initiation of individual record cards which will, at the end of a child's school life, have a complete statement of his progress in his school work but in addition will contain estimates of his personality development.

With the greater participation of the student in the learning process, it also follows that the incentives upon which learning is built will tend to move from constraints, external rewards like marks, prizes, ranking, towards mobilizing interest. If these things are true, then the way in which teachers are prepared has also to change. The methods of training can no longer be based upon the imparting of tricks of the trade but have to be transformed into a social education which primarily calls for, the development of an all-round approach to the pupil whereby a widened horizon and human understanding of the person become more important than the simple assessment of intellectual progress. The emphasis is now no longer on instruction and learning but rather on development of living. The educational institutions themselves have to become true societies and the course for the preparation of teachers has to be modified to take into account these changes.

It is for this reason that I wish to emphasize the historical and social changes which have transformed the narrower concept of education as related to training and instruction into something much broader and deeper which affects the personality of the pupil at all points and the relationship between the pupil and the teacher similarly. If I may refer back to the distinction which we drew earlier on between instruction, teaching and educating, I wish to reaffirm that educating must now represent the richest possible contact between persons and the recognition of the relationship between persons and the society in which they have grown up.

'The coat must be cut according to the cloth, but it must also be cut according to the would-be wearer.'

IV

The Historical Character of Educational Aims

SIMPLER and more traditional societies take themselves for granted and their educational aims and practices are relatively unquestioned—this happened for instance in England with relation to the classical curriculum in universities and schools for roughly four centuries. In a society which is more liable to change, those who have the historical perspective can become aware of the transitions which are taking place during their lifetime and in the larger span of historical time of which they are a part. People thus aware of change have to digest and assimilate the knowledge which is theirs through their education and to detect what are to become the important aspects of this knowledge. They have to prospect in ideas ahead of their time. They have to do all this without losing faith in what has been handed on to them from their past and what their contribution is going to be to the future.

Let us illustrate this point by making a brief survey of some of the educational aims and ideals which have established themselves in Western European history. All these theories (and those which will be mentioned are only some of the main ones) have this in common, that they are trying to transform what exists into something higher and better. They begin to show their differences when this higher aim has to be specified in some detail.

Consider, first, the Greek ideal. It will be impossible to give here much idea of the historical development over six or seven centuries of this ideal yet there is a general agreement that the main features of what we regard as characteristically Greek are to be found in the Athens of the fifth century B.C. and after. In earlier centuries a warrior aristocracy with a retinue of faithful followers fought for survival. Later this quasi-feudal organization became associated with the city states, where the free citizens of one state defended themselves from the others and from the invasions of the larger empires. Both Sparta and Athens in different ways had contributions to make to the ideal of the good life which we now regard as recognizably Greek.

There are two main features in this heritage, that of the soldier and that of the bard. The soldier reveals himself as a man of courage able to serve and yet wishing to excel with the deed of great bravery, physically beautiful and well proportioned. Later we find coupled with the virtues of the soldier those of the athlete. The heritage of the bard shows itself in the importance of music, gymnastic, dance, drama. To these two ancestries may later be added a third—we think of the Greek virtues as military and literary but also political. Excellence in council, the virtues of the politician and the ability to express and defend a point of view are admittedly Greek and with them goes the noble pride and love of freedom of the independent man.

In the hands of men like Socrates, Plato, Aristotle and Thucydides the notions of justice, simplicity, moderation, harmony, good faith become more explicit. The good man is identified with the good citizen and the good in itself is associated with the beautiful. We do not think of the Greek virtues as having much to do with asceticism or with indifference. Theirs are the virtues of enthusiasm and commitment and also of acceptance. Their gods are not supreme and righteous— indeed in Homer we find that they lie, they cheat and they commit adultery and Plato did not wish his philosopher-kings to be exposed to the corruption of having to read in Homer and in other poets of the defections of the gods. Yet moral goodness becomes one of the established principles of Greek civilization as we think of it now and this goodness is not the result of transcendental activity but the expression of human nature. It is the harmonious functioning of all the elements in human personality, and in this moderation is in all things ideal.[1]

The Roman ideal of the loyal and brave man is simpler and in a sense derivative—it has its ancestry perhaps more in

Sparta than in Athens. However the list of cardinal virtues in the ancient world of Greece and Rome might read something like this—justice, fortitude, prudence, temperance and individual pride.[2]

If we turn to the Hebrews we find first the assertion of one God who has made a covenant with His people and the cardinal virtue of the Hebrews is to seek holiness. As a chosen people the Hebrews developed a sense of history with themselves as the people through whom God speaks. Early in the Old Testament this god appears as a special version of a tribal deity. But as the message of the Old Testament develops the awareness that Jehovah is indeed the one God becomes more and more clear. Also in the Hebrew tradition is the notion that this one God communicates with men and that he will reveal himself even more fully through the Messiah when he shall come.

Just as the Greek ideal took many centuries to realize itself in the form which later ages have come to recognize as typical, so the Hebrew ideal of holiness is to be traced through more than a thousand years of their history as seen in the Old Testament. Christianity cannot properly be understood unless it is seen in the context of the mission and self-awareness of the Jewish people.

The Messiah was thought to be the one who shall redeem his people, who are by nature wicked and self-seeking. The Old Testament is full of instances of punishments served on a transgressing people by a severe Father who, while he is the God of love is also the God of wrath. Jesus Christ, the Christian Messiah, is a very different figure from the one expected to come in glory to redeem his people and to lead them in triumph over their enemies. The Christian ideal takes the Jewish principle of holiness and obedience and develops it beyond the chosen people to make it the option open to all God's creatures, Jew and Gentile alike. All are equal in the sight of God. The first shall become last and the last first. Jesus's attendants are not soldiers, scholars, statesmen or kings, but fishermen and ordinary workmen, for the most part. Redemption is to be achieved by this Messiah not through over-mastering power but through terrible meekness and the characteristic Christian virtues are faith, hope and love—but the greatest of these is love.

Although Christ is the Messiah in the Christian belief, he also has said to men, 'Be ye perfect even as your Father in Heaven is perfect.' He also left with his followers and with those who should come after, the Holy Ghost, the Comforter, in whose power it would be possible to be in some measure like the Messiah, although the essence of the Christian Messianic hope is that this act of Jesus Christ in becoming the Messiah is a once-for-all, discontinuous act. The resurrection story gave men a hope and a guarantee of life beyond the grave and salvation was to be gained when God had judged the good and the evil at some final consummation of his purpose at a Judgment Day beyond time and history. So the Christian viewpoint had a perspective beyond this world, and the means of salvation in the example and life of Christ in this world.

A thousand years or more after the death of Jesus Christ the Christian religion had taken many forms in different countries and the Church was the great institution of religion with its chief centres in Rome and Byzantium. Christianity in Europe had become associated with a certain kind of social structure which we call loosely feudalism. There are three main streams of thought which may be detected in medieval Christendom. The first expresses itself in the monastic tradition, in the asceticism of devoted monks whose spiritual duty is to serve God in prayer and contemplation. The monasteries had many social functions to discharge, not the least important of which was in education and in healing the sick and caring for the poor. But the monastic ideal, as we understand it now, is associated with the denial of the self and the offering up of the soul in prayer, contemplation and adoration. The hermit or the holy man are in the same mould and tradition. The monastery is essentially a classless society but those who serve God in this way recognize the need for a personal discipline and also for authority which is vested in the prior or the abbess, who yet is a servant of God and in that sense one with the humblest member of the monastic community.

The feudal system had within it a formalized structure of behaviour and right which we now call chivalry, and this is the second stream in medieval Christianity. Nobles have enforced upon them by reason of their birth and their responsibility a code of honour and behaviour toward their peers, their subordinates and towards women, which expresses the virtues of moderation and courtesy in a largely formal fashion. Deep set in the chivalric tradition is allegiance to the Church and the Christian faith. While it is true that chivalry is a form of expression characteristic of a caste system it has a direct relationship with religious belief but yet it is quite distinct from the monastic tradition mentioned above.

The third stream in medieval Christianity appears in the loyalty to the guilds and the ideals of craftsmanship and self-respect which they embodied. The guilds were the societies which built up and expressed the professional ideals of the merchants and the craftsmen in a way parallel to the chivalric ideals which served the noblemen. The system of apprenticeship carried with it the necessity for sound elementary knowledge and a growing mastery of the craft with the recognition that there were standards of workmanship and integrity in the membership of a guild. Here again the place and importance of the Church and of Christian ideals can be seen. Even the medieval universities to which we owe the development of higher education in its contemporary form in Europe were included in the guild system because the professor of a medieval university considered himself as a member of a corporation with a special code of honour and behaviour and so indeed did the undergraduate. The University of Bologna grew up on the system of government by the guild of students who appointed their Rector. The University of Paris on the other hand gave its responsibility for government to the guild of teachers. At its height medieval society had an order and symmetry in which religious ideals expressed themselves through the lives of the different orders in society, spiritual, aristocratic, civil and military. Many of our older educational foundations such as the universities of Oxford and Cambridge and the public schools like Eton and Winchester have their origins in this society.[3]

Perhaps the chief difference between a man of the High Middle Ages and one of the Renaissance is to be found in the source of authority upon which each relies in making judgments. The man of the Middle Ages has a church and a hierarchy of priesthood together with a relatively established social order to guide him—he has in fact clear indications from the world in which he lives as to the judgments which he could make. The Renaissance man relies far less on external authority and develops a form of self-confidence which in some cases may even be considered arrogance. He is in a sense a law to himself. He has to base his judgments on the effects his actions will have on other men. Here we find the beginnings of that concentration on phenomena of this world and the significance of personal experience which leads in a fairly direct line to the development of the scientific outlook of the seventeenth and eighteenth centuries. The scepticism which accompanied this outlook dissolves and changes the medieval world view. The society is no longer so clearly demarcated as it formerly was. Bankers, diplomats, scholars, painters, are now recognizable in their own independent right. The great man begins to supersede the religious and moral traditions of the mass of the people. In the Middle Ages, self-confidence could become very easily the sin of *superbia* or arrogance although *magnanimitas*, a largeness of mind and sympathy, was also appreciated. In the Renaissance times self-confidence was a recognized and approved assurance.

Here there is a fresh assessment of the place of man, the independence of his judgment and the role of leadership.[4] While the Middle Ages were never as settled as this over-simplified account of them would seem to suggest, it is true that they had a traditional orderliness which was broken up by the Renaissance. After this emerges the individualism which in theological terms becomes Protestantism. Here we have the transformation of an order of things which was accepted in medieval times and which in due course became the new cosmology where the earth was no longer the centre of all things but itself swam in a new empyrean of stars and planets. Theology was formerly the Queen of the Sciences but this was now no longer the case. The cardinal virtues of such a time were spiritual and intellectual courage which was bound to have as its obverse a fear of the loneliness which this new independence brought in its train.[5]

From roughly the sixteenth to the nineteenth centuries in England the men and women who surrounded the King or the Queen became an envied group. They had formal manners and depended on the favours of the sovereign for their standing and popularity at the court. The outward forms of courtesy had to be maintained and it depended very much on the interests of the sovereign as to whether there were any intellectual pretensions amongst his courtiers. It is seldom that the ideal courtier was expected to be intellectually notable, yet the orders of the nobility with the responsibilities that they carried in the country as owners and administrators of land had great influence on the lives of men and women who lived on their estates. In England the ideal of the gentleman which is in itself complex and of the greatest importance in national life has its origins in the court and its ways. So too has the chivalric ideal of the nobleman as a responsible ruler and landlord. If it has pleased God to call him into a superior position in society he has duties attendant upon his good fortune. Here too is an important strand in later educational practice in England.

In the U.S.S.R. at the present time we have a new kind of ideal, the chief characteristic of which is the willingness to submerge the self in the interests of the group. Marxism assumes that an egalitarian society is possible and that the whole of history is moving in that direction and has an inexorable inner compulsion to do so. At present the Communist Party is a minority movement in the democracies of the west and it has its example in the policies and procedures of Soviet Russia.

The collective ideal can be seen in the principles which are supposed to guide members of the Communist Party in Russia who are expected to be the leaders in social action. It is not sufficient to be simply a good group worker prepared to submerge your own interests, it is necessary also for each person to impose a strict personal discipline on his actions so that the work of the collective shall not be jeopardized by reason of his failure to fulfil his obligations. We have in this collective ideal at its best the notion of individual responsibility and good example on the one hand and on the other self-discipline and self-submergence in the interests of one's fellows.

*   *   *   *

In these very sketchy comments on some of the varying ideals which can be detected at different periods in history I have tried to show that a residue of attitudes, principles and forms of behaviour have been passed on from generation to generation and have mingled one with the other. It would be very difficult, for instance, to disentangle the various threads in the kind of ideal person which we have in mind as the best example by which to live at the present time. However, it would be helpful if we looked more closely at one of the very powerful patterns which have persisted in English education. I want to do this so that we can see how norms exist in our aspirations and ways of thinking even though these norms have to be re-defined in the passage of time. Let us consider the main phases in the development of the *gentleman ideal* which has persisted for a very long time in English culture.

The gentleman ideal is a composite product of medieval chivalry, of Renaissance humanism and of the upward progress of the middle classes in British history. The term is found first of all in English history in Latin documents of late medieval times where it appears as the word *generosus* meaning the man of good family and good social position who enjoys standing and esteem in the opinion of his fellows. It is confined at first to the class ideal of the knight or the peer and a mark of his standing is to be found in the outward symbol of the coat of arms which became the necessary mark of the gentleman. However, as time passed and social ranking became much more fluid and it was possible by reason of commercial success and worth-while service to the community to obtain the necessary recognition from the king—it was possible as time passed to buy this mark of social standing. One of the conditions of the gentleman's rank was that he had nothing to do with manual labour.

In England there did not exist a distinct class of gentlemen and in the early fifteenth century it is probable that the younger sons of noble families to whom land and possessions did not pass on the death of the father and who therefore could not remain on the land or who for one reason or another did not choose to, described themselves in certain legal documents as gentlemen in order not to sink in the social scale and be confused with the yeoman, the husbandman or the trader. There are in existence statutes of the early fifteenth century which allow this procedure and we have here an example of a new type of ranking in the hierarchy. Such gentlemen, however, were still related to the knights and the noble houses and they possessed and spread more widely into society the virtues characteristic of these groups. They were loyal to their sovereign as the conflicts within the nobility came to an end and there was some settled future to the kingship from the time of the Tudors onwards. After the establishment of the Anglican Church and the breakaway from Rome they were loyal through the sovereign to the church. They had a high ideal of personal honour to their own class and a studied reverence for women, also of their own class. Professor T. H. Marshall points out that while gentlemen and nobles tended to marry within their own class groupings it was known for them to marry beneath them and as he quotes, 'To marry beneath oneself is merely taking dung to manure one's acres'.[6]

It was characteristic of the gentleman that he should be generous in behaviour and that he should show in his appearance and his possessions a certain elegance, not to say flamboyance. His house was an indication of his standing and his dress and appearance had their importance also. It was expected that he would have as the centuries passed a sophistication associated with travelling and knowledge of other European countries, that he would in his younger day at any rate, be interested in physical pursuits and sport and should preferably be expert at them. It is easy to see from what has been said before that many of these virtues are similar to those found in medieval chivalry and in the Greek ideal. A gentleman was ready to give service to his equals and to his sovereign. He was not expected to have a vocation and he was supposed to be sufficiently well placed in possessions not to need to exercise noticeable thrift.

In the picture as it has been drawn so far there is no evidence of attention to education or intellectual attainment. The gentlemanly ideal in the sixteenth century was associated with birth and the noble houses. However in the sixteenth and seventeenth centuries the influence of merchants and bankers began to be felt in noble circles. Allied with this the influences of humanism also had their effect as education and manners came to be identified with people of position. William of Wykeham when founding Winchester College in the late fourteenth century had chosen as its motto, 'Manners makyth man' and this became the more obvious as a sign of the gentleman about two hundred years later.

Near the beginning of the seventeenth century we find that the status of gentlemen is much more fluid than ever before. Neither blood nor military achievement is now the only qualification but conformity to the pattern of what is required is much more obvious. All things should be done with courtesy and grace. Here again the Greek ideal of moderation reveals itself. Extremes were to be avoided and while learning was to be respected it was not to be given precedence. Intellectual excellence should be part of the gentleman's equipment but grace of behaviour and quality of character should be pre-eminent. The learned man had to give precedence to the gentleman and the nobleman, and at all costs pedantry and intellectualism were to be avoided. The gentleman may be the patron of the arts and later of the sciences but he should not himself be a practitioner.

Tolerance of the opinions of others was also a feature of the gentleman and when in the seventeenth century the extremes of Puritanism showed themselves the gentlemanly ideal was under attack. To the gentleman scepticism, or át least an attitude of acceptance, was approved and fanaticism was regarded as hateful. Even speaking the full truth directly became a mark of the uncivilized and barbarous person.

These canons of gentlemanly behaviour carried over into the domain of commerce and industry and for many people became a guiding principle in their commercial behaviour. They represent the ideals of fairness and common-sense moderation which were characteristic of just dealing. They had nothing to do with servility and self-effacement but more to do with self-reliance and personal integrity. The ideal of asceticism which as we have seen was associated with the monastic principle of the Middle Ages was not acceptable to the merchants and the bankers of the sixteenth and seventeenth centuries, or at least to those who were not Puritans.

As a consequence of this transference of behaviour characteristic of a minority group of gentlemen and nobles to the merchants and bankers, and indeed to the members of the learned professions, the class differences became blurred and instead of a recognizable but difficult to define group of persons called gentlemen, we find that later in the seventeenth century there has grown up a feeling common to a number of different groups in society, not simply to the gentlemen by birth. Perhaps the best way to characterize this new feeling is to call it the solidarity of the well bred.[7]

Even the aspiring artisan in the nineteenth century begins to feel that he may be able to have gentlemanly qualities because there has been a gradual extension during the eighteenth century, and the first half of the nineteenth, of the class idea. When Thomas Arnold speaks of the education of the Christian gentleman in the public school of the nineteenth century he has taken many of the virtues which we have seen appearing in the Middle Ages in the ideals of chivalry and in the notion of the responsible behaviour of the gentleman of the sixteenth and seventeenth centuries, and has gathered them together in the special context of nineteenth-century England.[8] He had in mind an ideal which imprinted itself upon the institution of the public school in such a way that it became an example for the grammar schools of England when they came into existence after 1902 when local education authorities were set up.

Here is a case of the spread of an ideal which is in itself complex, having many origins, to groups within a society very different from the groups with which the ideal was at first associated. Indeed the pattern itself has been changed and modified as new additions and new principles have been added with the passage of time. Even now in the middle of the twentieth century the English gentleman is a pattern and example for many people who would find it very difficult to define exactly what they meant. Nevertheless the influence of attitudes which we have tried very hastily to sketch has penetrated deeply into the moral consciousness of many different layers of English society.

For reasons like these, therefore, it is important to notice that current attitudes have historical antecedents, and that large-scale principles (for example, 'love one another' or 'be ye perfect'), have to be interpreted in historical terms which can differ very widely from one age to another. For instance it could be' argued that a Christian in these days following the precept 'love one another' regards all forms of warfare as being fundamentally contradictory to this principle. However, at the time of the Crusades, Christians regarded it as a sign of their loyalty to the Christian belief that they should wage war against those who did not share their faith.

We have to clarify our values and it is necessary to train our ability to disentangle the aims and ideals for which we are prepared to stand. It is not to be expected that through more and more factual analysis we can find the answer to all our value decisions. A curriculum laboratory in the United States of America collected fifty thousand curricula as practised in various schools. But it would not be possible to get the norm of what is being done or what ought to be done through trying to work out the averages of needs.

In our age it is not enough to say that this or that educational system or theory or policy is good. We have to determine *for what* it is good, for which historical aims it stands and whether we want this educational result. We may not be able to detect clearly all the consequences of what we are doing explicitly or implicitly through our educational activities but some we certainly can see and in these days of planning for freedom we should be aware of as many of these as possible.

In a democratic society fluidity in educational aims is a pre-condition to serving the interest of differing groups representing a variety of religious beliefs, of social classes, of nationalities, occupational groupings and even of races. We could not have arrived at the type of democracy which we now possess in Britain if there had not been a considerable intermingling of cultures and a necessary fusion at certain points. Because of the variety of ideal personalities, some of which have been sketched in this chapter, we can see that there is a wide tolerance in personality patterns. It is characteristic of British ways of thinking that we should want to see if a compromise might be possible when two points of view clashed. In education any claim to absoluteness would lead to fanaticism which is to be avoided in a rapidly changing society such as our own.

Nevertheless, there are large-scale aims and values of transcendent importance, and there are varying degrees of intermediate aims and purposes of a more transitory and immediate significance. For instance, Jesus's disciples wished to survive in order to spread the good news of the Gospel and in this is to be found the beginnings of the Christian Church spreading over the centuries. However, for this to take place the original disciples and their religious descendants had to make short-term judgments affecting their own lives and even their survival. As time passed this Christian group showed the features which are characteristic of any group which wishes to survive over a period of time. It had to have a certain common knowledge and agreed purpose, a unity and integration to which new-comers had to conform. In time this gives rise to a generalized attitude to the group which we call a tradition. As well as this, however, if the activity and influence of the group are growing, it has to work out means of increasing its knowledge, efficiency and skill. The occupational virtues follow and usually a division of labour and function ensues. Conflicts of interest are bound to grow up and aggressive impulses to arise between people and at this point the group has to have some means of dealing with these disintegrating factors. It is here that a sense of belonging to a movement which is larger than the persons immediately involved in it, stretching backwards through time and having a collective existence which goes on into the future, has a stabilizing effect.

What are the characteristic, pervasive aims of the present time which seem to stem from a long history of striving and clarification and in the other direction seem to point to a future to which most people would wish to commit themselves? First I should place the attempt to move towards a non-tyrannical structure of society, a democratic order in which the wishes of individuals were given due weight in relation to the wishes and needs of groups. Second, and arising out of the first, I should place the striving for a co-operative world organization which should operate without resort to war or violence as an attempt to solve differences. Once these large-scale aims of the age were accepted by a majority of people as binding, a great many intermediate values would follow from them. The cardinal virtues in a democratic order would show themselves to be a spirit of co-operation, a willingness to share responsibility and a respect for the views of others arising out of greater tolerance. This tolerance may take two forms. First the willingness to accept a point of view which has hitherto been unacceptable and second, while understanding another point of view, being prepared to continue to differ but with a deeper sympathy. Such liberal attitudes would give a greater dignity and freedom to all people and much more general access to knowledge and information. On the other hand within such a framework there are values on which such general agreement cannot be reached. For instance if we consider property rights, should a person be free to own and dispose of his property without restraint or should there be some common responsibility for the ownership of property, perhaps even private property with public control? Here of course issues which have been considered by economists from Adam Smith to Marx are in question. The democratic virtues raise the important issue of changing attitudes toward competition, rivalry, the degree of individuality, attitudes towards the position of the classes and the importance of status and ambition.

On the plane of world co-operation we are faced with the value system of an intense nationalism in the younger nations competing with the desire for world government and a central organization. Even here the large power blocks are divided into sectional interests. The mid-way step in these conflicts of interest seems to be to follow a policy of containment as far as the basic conditions of survival go, to seek to avoid war and aggressiveness on a large scale as much as possible and on smaller issues to agree to differ if they do not interfere with such co-operation as can be achieved. In fact what we are seeing here is a tendency to regard the large-scale values as very faint guide lines and to proceed step by step to pick our way through the immediate problems.

To have an aim or a purpose is to choose between values and to persist in one's choice. This is true whether it applies to politics or education. The large-scale ideal aims as I have tried to show are influenced by the context of historical time. What could be achieved by education, whether in terms of knowledge or the type of character which it should help to produce, was necessarily different in medieval England from today. The achievement of an integrated system of values at any time in history can be obtained only through choices between competing values.[9]

V

Individualism and the Sociological Approach to Education

M ANY people consider that it is the individual who is the moving force of history, the source of all values and the initiator of events. Without his contribution, society would be a matter of mechanical organization and so the individual should be the hinge in all our social plans.

Sir Percy Nunn expressed this point of view in education:

'What, then, could education do better than to strengthen men's sense of the worth of individuality—their own and others'—teaching them to esteem the individual life, not, indeed, as a private possession, but as the only means by which real value can enter the world?'[1]

There is of course nothing wrong in wanting to help in the development of personality but to speak in these terms without any reference to circumstances makes this notion an empty concept. To be fair to Nunn, however, the rest of his book contains a far fuller treatment of the context than this quotation would suggest. But as Sir Fred Clarke said of it, it showed signs of society blindness and did not seem to be sufficiently aware of the fact that society around us indicates and limits our potentialities much more than we realize and than Nunn seemed disposed to admit.

At the other extreme to individualism we have those who believe that the only important developing entity is either the nation or the society and that the inner forces controlling its growth can be detected. This means a predetermined social and historical process in which persons participate, not as abstract

47

personalities but as social beings who are part of a collective history. This, of course, is the characteristic view of the Marxist and to him the aim of education is to help everyone to find his place, his function and his fulfilment in the process of history.

This idea is found in Hegel at the beginning of the nineteenth century. He said that the state was a super-personal entity of which the single life is but a fugitive element. The state is an age-long spiritual life from which the individual spirit with its own private will and conscience draws whatever measure of reality it possesses. Such a view is not society-blind as Clarke claimed that Nunn's was. Hegel maintains that personal ideals emerge out of the historical context in which people live and each age helps to define the scope of activities and the potentialities which may be developed at that time. Nevertheless there is a rigidity about this point of view because the progress of the state is predetermined and no alternative possibilities can be entertained; a strict regimentation follows characteristic of all totalitarian schemes. The historical setting is not considered here as a field in which personality can grow and develop but as a framework of constraint which shapes and moulds what it may become.

So there is a characteristic one-sidedness in each of these two perspectives. The individualists regard education as a process of interaction between individuals who may easily be regarded as separate ends in themselves (it is fair to say that Nunn tries to counteract this danger). The effect of education is visible in and to individuals. Education is concerned with effecting a change in the knowledge and attitudes of a person and its success can only be measured in this way. The eye of the collectivist, on the other hand, is upon the progress and change taking place in the society. He does not regard the individual as the main object of his inquiry. What is happening to the society is what interests him and education is simply a method by which the collective trains the new generation for predetermined functions and particularly for citizenship. The horizon of probabilities for each person is neglected.

These two perspectives do not exist in the stark opposition in which I have outlined them. However, their inner tendencies are as I have indicated. There is a third way which integrates the valuable elements in both schemes. According to this view an individual is not an abstracted personality but develops as a social self in the society which exists at a certain time in history. His potentialities have to be detected as talents which may be employed in ways which are satisfying to him and of value to the community. He will make creative contributions both by himself as a person and in his co-operative efforts. Society is not a mechanism out of which the individual makes his own life. It is the stuff out of which a large part of his very self is woven.

The educational consequence of this point of view is that a progressive society depends upon the development of differentiated personalities who recognize their responsibility to the community to which they belong and make their contributions as best they may with the talents which they possess. Equal attention is then given to the spontaneity of the person and to the significance of the environment in which this person grows. This is what we mean by a democratic order—the society which recognizes the need for discipline together with the maximum flexibility for the individual choice. John Dewey put it in this way:

'But since society can develop only as new resources are put at its disposal, it is absurd to suppose that freedom has positive significance for individuality but negative meaning for social interests. Society is strong, forceful, stable only when all its members can function to the limit of their capacity.'[2]

The more we realize the educative power of our environment the more we are driven to revise some of our main concepts concerning man. Not only a great part of his behaviour which formerly seemed to be innate or inherited proves to be the result of learning and an inter-play between himself and the world around him. But even his individuality, his self, his personality, seems to develop out of this interaction. His higher learning, his ability for abstract thought develops out of an elaboration of much simpler processes, such as infantile conditioning—in fact the way to learn has to be learned as an infant grows into a child and to an adult.

Therefore in our educational thinking we must become aware of the need to clarify our ideas of the growth of personality. We have to place far less reliance on our previous image

49

of man as a being with innate ideas and an inherited ready-made sacrosanct personality. Even while we may be prepared to revere the person as an end in himself, as a creative moral being, as Kant suggests,[3] we have to balance this with a readiness to see how this person, born at a certain stage in time, of parent stock, part of a nation with a history, has come to grow up with his psychological endowment and sociological surroundings to be the person that he is.

*   *   *   *

So we end this first section concerned with theoretical and sociological matters related to the aims of education. We have tried to see so far that education has narrower and broader definitions and that a person grows up with a heritage of ideas and values which are as much a part of his personal equipment as the instruction which he receives. Similarly the society to which he belongs has itself typical contemporary problems in which he will be required to engage. These problems express in a particular form the phase which man has reached in his dealings with things and forces in nature and with other men. The long-term aims in education express values which men will continue to choose as the guide lines in their behaviour as they try to transform what is into something which is higher.

In our consideration of the relationship between sociology and education we must now turn to the psychological problems with which we must deal.

PART TWO

PSYCHOLOGICAL MATTERS

VI

The Flexibility of Human Nature and
Social Conditioning

ANTS and bees form societies as we know and even have
a division of labour and a kind of state with a clear
differentiation of function. However, they go on generation after generation reproducing the same kind of social
patterns and therefore, unlike man, they have no history. They
adapt themselves to situations by inherited behaviour patterns
which we call instincts whilst man no longer inherits these fixed
forms of behaviour which provide the ants and the bees with
ready-made patterns of adjustment. While the human infant
starts life with simple and clear needs that have to be satisfied,
not unlike the simple, clear instincts of the ants and the bees,
the baby as he grows is compelled to acquire a wide range of
new behaviour patterns which he has the endowment and
flexibility to encompass and which are quite beyond the range
of the lower animals. Dr. Johnson had this in mind when he
pointed out that it needed twenty-three years to produce a
curate but it takes a very few minutes to have a chicken ready
to get on in life. The chicken has inherited or instinctive mental
patterns for the few tasks it has to fulfil and it needs a very small
amount of learning to discharge these, whereas a human infant
is born helpless with a very few fixed instinctual patterns and
he needs a long training and education in order to acquire the
most important patterns of behaviour.

Nevertheless, in spite of these differences, man and the
lower animals are in the same case in so far as life to both of them
is a series of adjustments to their changing environment and
as each has behaviour patterns at its disposal, but in the case of

53

man these are so pliable that a wide scope for variation in experience and learning is open to him. In any society as he grows he finds the institutions of great importance in shaping his response—and by institutions is meant accepted forms of behaviour, accepted rules or criteria which have been fixed by history and tradition, like the institutions of marriage, family, school.

Man has made his progress in history because he has transferred from one generation to the next the best forms of adjustment—the most successful ways of living. He has been able to do this because he has had a greater command of the medium of learning than has been available to any of the lower animals. You can inherit through the biological medium, through the germ plasm, a certain physique, your basic vitality and the means of seeking survival but you cannot inherit the content of a culture in this way. We know that skill and knowledge acquired during lifetime are not transferred to our descendants through the biological inheritance—as an obvious example, if you learn typewriting your children do not inherit this skill from you. They may in their turn learn the skill, but this is because they have been active to acquire it for themselves. The results of learning in one generation are not passed on to and passively acquired by the next.[1] Effective learning takes place only where in response to a felt need a person takes active hold on some part of his environment, some ideas, habits, skills and weaves them into a new pattern of behaviour for himself.

This learning process which is the greatest achievement of human beings as compared with the lower animals, starts anew in each generation, indeed in each infant, as it grows. It is for this reason that all racial theories can be disproved because such theories consider that culture is to be inherited and transmitted by the race in its germ plasm, whereas in fact it is acquired in the lifetime of the individual and passed on from generation to generation through language, habit, tradition and imitation. However, these distinctively human qualities have grown out of man's ability to transform his inherited biological potentialities into culture patterns. This is why whenever our social institutions and our personal life are radically disturbed, we so easily regress to the naked instinctual tendencies obvious in the lower animals—we can see it in time

54

of war, in famine, in bitter poverty. It is probably true to say that as to our biological constitution man is not very different from his cave-man ancestors. In terms of social inheritance, however, there is scarcely any comparison.

INSTINCTS AND HABITS

In ordinary speech we very often use the words habit and instinct as though they were interchangeable. People speak of a property instinct, a criminal instinct, when they really mean to refer to habits which have been acquired and not to something which is innate.

We build up our habits on the basis of experience and learning. They are mostly complex but grow from simple instinctual tendencies, just as our complex movements which have become habitual and unnoticed are based on the random and chaotic movements of the new-born baby. You can see what I mean if you think of the behaviour of an infant who waves his hand about and moves his fingers in a simple and apparently purposeless way. Some years later the same infant may begin to learn to play the piano and to build up a series of complex movements which have grown up as extensions of the earlier random waving of the hand. Through practice and learning he begins to develop new habit systems and as his skill grows these become as automatic, as unnoticed as were his infantile random movements. However, if he goes to a new teacher who considers that he has been learning bad musical habits, it is possible for the boy to break down his acquired movements and to re-examine the elements of what he has been doing and to learn a new way. Admittedly this is difficult and very often repugnant to a pianist who has achieved already a certain measure of success and there would be a good deal of emotional resistance to it. In fact one of the purposes of habit is that the movements should become automatic so that no thought is necessary for them and thus the conscious thinking part of the mind is free to deal with new problems which will need care and preparation and conscious application.

Of course we build up habits not only on the plane of physical movements and simple reactions, but on higher levels too. For instance we have from our infancy been taught different ways of eating, different habits and time schedules of sleeping and all the manners and conventions which go with excretion. What we commonly call manners are themselves a series of habitual reactions based upon conventional behaviour. Ultimately, mental habits, such as shyness, ambition, greed, various forms of fear, are just as much acquired and conditioned in the span of our life as is the habit of using a fork, although the conditioning in the latter case of course is far simpler.

While it is true that habits represent an economy of effort, that they save our mental energies by freeing us from the necessity to invent all our responses anew from minute to minute, yet it should be remembered that if our situation changes, then there is nothing worse than a rigid habit which has been so familiar that it is not now possible to change it to meet the new conditions. In a time like the present when there are so many rapidly-changing situations, there is great need to keep our habit-making mechanisms under review. As Dewey said, 'What is necessary is that habits be formed which are more intelligent, more sensitively percipient, more informed with foresight, more aware of what they are about, more direct and sincere, more flexibly responsive than those now current.'[2]

Enough has been written by Pavlov and by others reporting on Pavlov and his dogs to make us thoroughly familiar with the notion of the conditioned reflex. The important point to notice here is the principle of association. What is conditioned is an association with another object or stimulus which in turn becomes a substitute for the original stimulus to the instinctive response. So the bells, the ellipses, the circles, represent the means by which through association of stimuli the dogs could multiply their experience and their responses. Hence, building upon our instinctive endowment, by association we can extend the whole range of our understanding.

Clark L. Hull has said that there are four fundamentals in learning. There is the *drive*, which is an innate or even acquired strong impulse to action (this is very close to what many people mean by instinct); then there is the *cue* which is the stimulus to the *response* or initiative on the part of the learner. For instance the whistle is a signal or a cue for the workman to throw down his tools and get out his lunch. The national anthem is the cue for appropriate learned behaviour, the response.

Finally there is the *reward* which marks the culmination or satisfaction of the drive itself.[3]

An obvious example of a powerful confusion of the idea of instinct and habit can be seen in race prejudice. We know that white and coloured children play easily together and that attitudes of avoidance are encouraged by the adults. As time passes, if there is a consistent hostility to people with different coloured skins, it becomes reasonable to expect that a child will have built up an automatic prejudice, the origins of which will be forgotten but which will be so deep-seated that we can believe it to be innate. It is here that we see how many of the different aspects of social life, the institutions in fact, have worked together to produce a psychological result which is so powerful that we are prepared to consider it as innate. Indeed one of the ways of strengthening and perpetuating the idea is to adopt the psychological determinism implied by the notion of race prejudice as an instinct.

In our educational efforts we have to recognize the existence of conditioning. For instance, it depends on the nature of the society and the social group in which we have been brought up, whether we feel favourably to such words as England, Nazi, Communist, bourgeois. By the same token we find that we have certain deeply ingrained notions of what constitutes good manners, respect for property and right moral behaviour. It is interesting to note that social anthropologists and sociologists have shown how standards in such matters vary, not only between nations but also between different social groups within the same nation. There is much truth in the idea that as these basic reactions are acquired in early childhood and adulthood builds upon this, the establishing of correct habits, or at any rate desirable habits, is a very important part of education— perhaps even more important than the building up of abstract ideals. By this I do not mean that we should undervalue higher intellectual processes but it is obviously imperative to see that the basic human values are established early in the life of a child. We decide which are to be the correct habits on the basis of the kind of person we would like to see this child become. This is a matter partly of moral philosophy, partly of psychology and partly of sociology. Of course 'correct' habits are a problem for adults as well as children.

Besides the conditioning of reflexes, Pavlov also spoke of deconditioning and reconditioning.[4] Although our social training gives a certain pitch and direction to our original nature we must recognize that there are some universal and basic drives which provide the foundation for our adult motives. There is an important difference of emphasis in the approach to this problem by dynamic psychologists and behaviourists. If we take psychoanalysts as an example of the dynamic psychologists we can examine these points of view more closely. It is of course true to say that there is a variety of opinion in detail within the psychoanalytic school and within the behaviourist school but certain common features can be detected.

Psychoanalysts maintain that there are two main fundamental drives in all human beings. The self-assertive or aggressive impetus and the sexual or social impetus. These act like innate tendencies and press in a certain direction to find some means of expression, some satisfaction. This concept is dynamic in the sense that the drives contain energy which, even if it is suppressed (and some of the energy is taken up in the act of suppression) will work in some way in the psychic economy of the person. In other words there is a recognizable initiative provided by these drives which is given shape and direction by the opportunities for expression in the environment.

The behaviourists believe that there are three innate emotional patterns, fear, rage and joy. Upon the basis of these three emotions a person's psyche may be built up by the forms of experience and the sorts of conditions in which they may be expressed. It may appear at first sight as if this is not very different from the psychoanalytic viewpoint and is in a sense dynamic. The main difference may be seen in the interpretation of learning. To the behaviourist learning takes place in a cumulative fashion and can be arranged for by the application of the principle of association. If we accept fear, rage and joy as the emotional states which we experience from infancy, then we may arrange conditions so that one or other of these feelings is called out and associated with the situation in which the infant finds himself. As one writer puts it:

'Parts may be thought of as the substances out of which wholes are made. Houses are made of bricks and wood and plaster, the whole is composed of all its parts so conceived—no more, no less.

Alternatively a whole may be thought of as a unique pattern or organization of the parts in which case the whole has properties beyond those of its parts or is 'more' than its parts. Thus a house has an architectural unity which is 'more' than the materials of which it is composed.'[5]

These alternatives—considering the whole as composed of separate parts which may be added on to the others until the object is complete, or considering wholes as a finished product organized in a certain way without the emphasis upon the individual parts—represent an important difference in the point of view of the associationist and of the psychoanalyst. To the associationist complex habits are elaborations and combinations of simpler habits involving new bonds or conditioned responses. These responses are made possible by the strength of the emotional conditioning aroused—that is to say the rage, fear or joy which have been called up by the various experiences. It is possible of course to decondition and recondition by calling upon emotions of fear where previously there had been a positive feeling, and reintroducing the positive feeling with a new association.

Watson, the best known and most extreme of the early behaviourists, gives an account of the way in which children may respond favourably to animals like rats which perhaps later in life they would expect to be afraid of. He has one much-quoted example of the child who is fond of a rabbit and then is frightened at the same time as the rabbit appears and at a later stage rejects it. Still later, however, the child's affection for the rabbit is re-established by a new conditioning procedure. Critics of the behaviourists' viewpoint call their preference for describing the whole according to its parts a form of atomism which has been borrowed from the outlook of nineteenth-century physical scientists.[6]

Psychoanalysts on the other hand tend to emphasize the readiness of an infant to respond with aggressive or social tendencies to the situation with which he is confronted. The fear or the rage or the joy which the child experiences is not simply an emotion which can be conditioned by the presentation of suitable stimuli, it is part of the response of the whole infant to his surroundings. Psychoanalysts are much more concerned, as we shall see later, with the processes of transferring what they call *libido* to various objects and persons than they are with the learning process. However, if we couple their viewpoint, which is concerned with the response of the whole person, to the attitude of those who are called *gestalt* psychologists we find a complementary interest.

The gestaltists emphasize the wholeness of experiences even from infancy. They are interested in the ways in which children learn, and indeed their theory of learning is indistinguishable f om a theory of behaviour—which also may be said of the behaviourists. The whole is more than a sum of the parts and this represents a viewpoint on all experience for the gestaltist. One of the commonest illustrations of this is that a melody is more than the tones and intervals of which it is composed. It has an internal relationship and sequence of musical ideas and this relationship is as much a part of the melody as the separate notes. A musical theme of this kind can be transposed into another key and maintain its structure and so too can material learned on one occasion, if this material can be of use in solving a new problem. Indeed the whole question of problem-solving is critical in estimating the differences between the behaviourists and the gestaltists.[7]

When we are faced with a new situation the gestaltists say that from our experience a number of related situations are called to mind at once, seeking to establish the connection between what we already know and this incomprehensible novelty. We do not run through all that we know in relation to the novelty. Or to put it another way, this new situation does not stimulate the related experiences in our past knowledge, which would seem to be the behaviourist's interpretation of what is happening. We as persons with a certain background of knowledge are striving in such a situation to apply what the gestaltists call the *closure* which will cause the new experience to be comprehended in terms of what we already know and as we would say *understood*. The parts do not add up to a whole in a cumulative way; the intuition of the whole, the closure, is experienced and then at a later stage we may look at the experience and isolate out the parts for examination. In fact the gestaltists are reversing the associationists' procedure. We shall consider this matter more closely when we deal with learning in greater detail.

Dynamic psychologists believe that psychological energy is expressed as emotion, as cognition and as action or a tendency to act. In different ways these ideas are to be found in McDougall, in Freud and in Burt.[8] Instinct to them is the name for the basic energy which is expressed in these ways. Freud has given this the name *libido*, although he has a number of special qualifications which we need not consider here but which he regards as indispensable to psychoanalytic thought. Associationists do not seem to have any such theory of the transformation of psychological energy into its various forms. It would appear that they lay emphasis upon reactions, particularly upon movements and response and the association of feeling with response in such a way as to set up pleasurable or unpleasurable psychological states. What we might call thinking as a form of mental activity with an inner compulsion of its own which may be deduced from the theories of the dynamic psychologists, is not to be found in the same way in associationist theory. It would appear that thinking arises from a more and more complicated mechanism of stimulus-response bonds. Associationists do not talk a great deal about perception but prefer to discuss this in terms of discriminatory reactions.

The heart of the matter is that associationists do not admit subjective or introspective experience as evidence. For them a psychology based upon the associations of neural response is to be relied upon much more than one based partly on the interpretation of subjective states and ideas. A psychology based upon the response of an organism is bound to be different from one which regards the organism as able to initiate its own activity and not simply to react to the stimuli to which it is exposed.

The psychic energy postulated by psychoanalysts is an analogue of the ability that man has to transform his biological inheritance into a culture which we have already mentioned. The notion here is that the infant is born with certain elementary needs for food, excretion and sleep and the drives which support the gratification of these are the self-assertive and the social tendencies. As the infant grows and matures, his nervous mechanism becomes sufficiently complex for him to encompass responses that are more elaborate than the simple physical satisfactions which were necessary at first, though these of course have to continue to be satisfied. As we have already said association of experiences and conditioning of response is the principle which is accepted by psychoanalysts as by behaviourists. However, psychoanalysts go on to say that as an infant develops, the drives to self-assertion and socialization express themselves in many different ways, which to some extent the infant himself can initiate though in other ways he is responding to what he sees about him and which he may accept more or less unwittingly.

The psychoanalyst has named many different forms of deflection or reinterpretation of the instincts of the infant and many of these are already well known. For instance *projection*, the mechanism by which we put on to others emotional states which we do not wish to admit in ourselves: or *rationalization*, the means by which we justify behaviour which contradicts the principles which we are supposed to hold dear. It is important to draw a distinction between this kind of self-deception and the sort of decision in which the person recognizes that he is having to choose a course of action of which he does not wholly approve but which he may consider to be the lesser of two evils. Of course it is possible to see even this psychological dilemma as being maybe a rationalization in itself. As motivation is seldom single and clear there must be plenty of examples of potential rationalizations though only those who are very close to each situation can tell how deliberate and clear-sighted a decision may be and how much self-righteous reasons are being given for something which may have very dubious motives indeed.

A transformation which takes socially approved form is called by the psychoanalyst *sublimation*. Obviously this mechanism is of great importance to education and represents a redirection of potentially destructive or socially unacceptable motives to better purposes. Freud is inclined to believe that sublimation is preceded and made possible by the process of *identification*, by which he means taking over largely unconsciously the behaviour, the attitudes and perhaps the appearance of an admired person. Obviously with small children the example might be one or other of their parents or a teacher or a brother or sister and psychoanalysts have made many suggestions as to the different phases of development in which identification is likely to appear. Certainly the quality of the relationship between an infant and his mother in particular is of the greatest significance for his later development.

Psychoanalysis also gives some account of many other mental processes in which the libido is deflected such as displacement, repression, introjection, reaction formation. There is no need here to try to particularize the meaning of these different responses. The important point is that in this dynamic psychology there is a recognition that a person is responding to his environment partly by his own initiative, that the experiences which he is having are being stored up at a conscious or unconscious level, however we may interpret the terms, and through these experiences a personality is coming into being, an individual with an experience which is his own, with which he lives and out of which he makes himself. We shall return to this whole difficult matter when we later try to deal with the essential aspects of personality development.[9]

This chapter has been about the flexibility of human nature and the whole concept of conditioning. We have had to give some attention to what we mean by instincts and habits. It has not been my intention to try to give a detailed account of developmental psychology. What I am trying to do is to show that in psychological thinking we have two main viewpoints, one of which says that man is unique as a learner in that he can initiate responses and transform to an unprecedented degree the tendencies he has inherited from his forebears. Yet even in this school of thought there has been an increasing recognition of the influence of a social environment. If Freud tended to emphasize the genetic aspects of psychology, his successors, like Horney, Sullivan, Kardiner, Erikson and Fromm,[10] have extended the whole field of reference of this method. The other viewpoint has stressed man as a neural mechanism set in an environment. Perhaps it would be truer to say that man is here considered as an organism and must not be given the special privileges of self-consciousness and must not start off with the advantage of appearing to possess a unique ability to initiate response. At the extreme of this wing of psychological thought is to be found Watson who challenges the validity of the whole concept of consciousness itself. Thorndike[11] and Hull differ from Watson in a number of particulars but they, together with

63

others like Guthrie[12] and Skinner,[13] have tried to develop a descriptive system of the learning process in terms of reinforcement, blockage, response and reward. This descriptive system does not concern itself with the personal possession of experience, with what I as a person make out of the experience which I am undergoing in my life. Yet in this approach to psychology, too, we find that there is increasing attention to the kind of environment which is providing the stimuli to which the human organism responds. Dollard and Miller[14] have written of this in their study of frustration and aggression and in a different sense Allport with his theory of functional autonomy provides a very useful bridge between the dynamic psychologists who stress the uniqueness of the learner and the associationists who describe the learning process as a system. Allport in his book on personality brings together aspects of each of these ways of thought in the most valuable synthesis.[15] Woodworth with his concept of the 'mental set' has introduced a notion of dynamic quality into a descriptive system, for over the years he has also had a great deal to say of the stimulus-response theories.[16]

Education is concerned with man the initiator, man the learner and the environment in which he learns, together with the purposes which that environment throws up to influence what he shall learn. There is as yet no authoritative psychology, no reliable system of explanation, but the two extremes of interpretation which I have indicated in this chapter show the polarities within which an increasingly coherent account might be expected.

VII

Learning

THE traditional view of learning was simply the acquiring and piling up of knowledge, the memorizing and knowing of facts. This of course raises very many problems of motivation and effectiveness which have to be considered if one is to get any kind of idea of learning from the point of view of the learner. The lower animals and humans all learn in some way or other, but for our purposes we will consider only human learning.

What happens when learning takes place? First the learner is aware of some obstruction to a need of his and hence of some dissatisfaction within himself. As a consequence he experiences a direct urge towards a goal—it may be the response of the infant who is hungry and cries to be fed, or the schoolboy working at a translation under the glowing eye of his teacher, or a researcher faced with an intractable problem which he must solve if he is to get any further in his investigation. This readiness to react is fundamental to learning but it is also the main characteristic of any behaviour by an adaptable organism. There is more to learning than just a readiness to react. After all, the learner may respond to the blockage with which he is faced but may not seem to be able to remove it—the infant may go on crying, the boy may not make sense out of his Latin prose, the researcher may try many different methods of solving his problem and not be able to.

The second step is that learning should be *successful* adaptive achievement, that as a result of the response and reaction the blockage and the dissatisfaction have been removed and positive feelings of achievement have been aroused. The emotional stress which provided some of the incentive to go on dealing with the situation changes to satisfaction and pleasure when the lesson has been learned or the problem solved.

The third feature of learning is that it must be *retained*, it must be available for recall and use. In order that this should happen the learner has to be aware of the relationship between what he now knows and the steps which have led up to it. This perception of relationships can vary from the rudimentary understanding of the infant who realizes that being lifted is probably a prelude to being fed, or the limited understanding of the schoolboy whose teacher points out that in the sentence in front of him he is having to deal with an ablative absolute, to the flash of insight of the researcher who sees a new way to deal with his problem. An increase in learning implies a greater facilitation of understanding. The hallmarks of successful learning are greater efficiency, economy and ease in dealing with new problems of the same kind, whether rudimentary or complex.

Much of the learning of young children is not deliberate but is rather a passive acceptance of experiences which, as we say, they have picked up. For instance, the random vocalization of the baby is the preparation for the deliberate speech of a later stage; posture and movement are also gradually acquired in this random way. So are the casual gestures of parents and others—the shrugs of the shoulders, the facial expressions and the tones of voice. Language is a very good example of what some psychologists call passive learning, at any rate in the early stages where sounds are made which gradually become associated with specific objects. As the need for communication becomes more complicated, so the need for a language more actively learned also grows. Passive learning represents the cultural conditioning upon which deliberate learning is based. A great deal of our teaching in the family serves as a background for more deliberate learning. A key notion in the transition from passive to active learning is motivation, the recognition of a purpose, and the emotions accompanying this purpose are of the greatest importance in giving to the learner what we call interest and a determination to pursue the learning through intervening frustrations. While it is true that human beings, like other animals, learn sometimes by random methods, they get a greater understanding and grasp when learning is the

66

result of purpose and interest and modern teaching method emphasizes the initiative of the learner.

Social approval and disapproval are obviously very potent factors in human motivation. It is in this way that a culture most strongly influences the learning of individuals. At an early stage the forms of encouragement or taboo help to lay down the limits within which an infant's responses are to take place. Psychologists who emphasize conditioning and early habit formations point out that very often our emotional responses and attitudes have been established at a non-voluntary level early in our lives—for instance, fear of the dark or more recently the failure to give and receive affection which has been isolated as of enormous importance. We can see in such instances as these how the dynamic psychology of Freud and the associationist approach of Hull can together give a much more satisfying account than each of them apart.[1]

Learning is a matter of continuous growth, we know, and it must obviously wait upon the physical maturation of the child —an infant in the first few months of life has not the manual dexterity to handle a spoon: his teeth, lips and tongue are not ready to produce language: the unbroken voice of a young boy prevents him from singing the bass part in a choir. But this growth of learning is not necessarily sequential and certainly not logical. It may proceed sometimes randomly or by trial and error or by insight and intuition, a leap of perception which finds the answer without being able to detect the steps by which it has been reached. There is also the routine procedure of logical continuity, the building up of knowledge step by step. A good instance of learning by trial and error occurs at parties when we are faced with one of those metal puzzles in which two pieces of metal are intertwined and we are expected to disentangle them. If we watch anyone trying to do this we notice that he looks at the pieces to see how they are tangled and after much thought and trying to analyse the problem, manipulating the pieces this way and that, at some point he seems to give up and simply to twist the pieces and pull at them, hoping for the best. He knows that there is a solution and he hopes that by some chance he will find it and maybe by tracing back what he has done, discover how he has done it.

The form of learning known as the conditioned response or

reflex is different from insight and logic in that it is a specific form of learning from which all errors have been eliminated by the use of a stimulus which is intended to produce the response with its attendant satisfaction directly. This response may then be reinforced by repetition of the stimulus.

While teachers are urged to encourage the initiative of the pupil and to give him opportunities for exercising insight or independent logical thought, it must be admitted that a great deal of teaching is of the order of conditioned response. For instance when we present a method of adding or subtracting, we are seeking to establish a means by which problems of this kind may be dealt with. In fact we select the examples so that the method we are teaching can be pursued without the awkward difficulties which more advanced examples might provide. We reinforce the performance of the child by giving him marks or ticks, or in some other way presenting him with a reward. In so far as we say to children at any point 'this should be done in this way' and offer no other opportunity for exploration or inquiry, we are conditioning a response, or to use other terminology we are indoctrinating the child, and there is nothing scandalous in admitting that this is the case. Gestaltists would argue that each problem that the pupil tries to solve is a new example of learning by wholes and into this argument I do not wish to enter. What is important is that very often we present only one method of solving a problem on the assumption that if we present more we shall only confuse our pupils and in so far as we do not expect the method to be questioned we are relying upon the conditioned response.

Consider for a moment the barrage of new inter-relationships which an infant has to face as he grows. He has to arrange his conduct in response to situations like the following—those which have to do with feeding, both the times and diet and the mother feeding him. He has toys to manage and manœuvre, from which he can learn much in the way of sense experience. He has to master times and places for and conduct suitable to, defaecation and urination: also there is the matter of clothes, what should be worn, how it should be worn and later, when it should be worn. Living in a house the infant has to learn a great deal about other people's possessions and ways of dealing with furniture, utensils and decorations, as well as drinking in impressions at all times from this, his most intimate surrounding. In a house and home we lay the foundations of an outlook toward things of beauty, tidiness, comfort, spaciousness, living with others in a large family or having a room to oneself, and so on.

Language is perhaps the most useful instrument of all to acquire and it is built up through the years of infancy on what the members of our family, friends, and acquaintances teach us deliberately or which we acquire unwittingly as infants. The habits of the home toward language are very likely to be the habits of the child and the sort of language that is used in the home and which is associated with loved ones, becomes the kind of language which the child wishes to use himself. Ideas very often run on ahead of articulateness and it is a common experience to find a three- or four-year-old child frustrated by his own verbal inadequacy. On the other hand the household which is laconic or conversationally poverty-stricken will also set a pattern for an infant growing up in it.

The objects of danger are usually made known to an infant early on and his behaviour has to be regulated accordingly. At a later stage these objects may cease to be causes of fear and avoidance but rather challenges and he must arrange his behaviour according to what he himself wishes to do and what he knows will be allowed.

Here we come to the very difficult matter of etiquette, whether it has to do with the outward forms of behaviour toward parents, relatives or strangers, or whether it has to do with competing standards—as for example when small boys dare one another to do things which they know their parents would forbid and which they would not try to do in their presence. The form of self-control or self-assertion appropriate to the setting in which you find yourself is often very difficult to discern and appropriate behaviour is learned only over a considerable period. Some habits of etiquette are often established very early—for instance, the deference which a Victorian child had to give to his father was never questioned in infancy and childhood and only with great pain in many cases was it called into question later.

Then there are the attitudes of mind appropriate for different situations—those which have to do with religion or punishment are supposed to be treated with solemnity. There are occasions for sadness and sorrow where humour would be quite out of the question, there are others where elation is free to express itself.

And so we could go on. A growing child has to take his cue on what is expected from him from the surroundings in which he is placed. The culture persuades, coerces and restrains him in his behaviour and quite often he has little choice in the matter and is not responsible for deciding the sort of behaviour which he should adopt in any spontaneous sense. While a great deal of this is much less true in our days than used to be the case, the heart of the matter is that we grow up with a large number of attitudes which have been accepted in our formative years unwittingly, and necessarily so.

The greatest of man's achievements in learning is his ability to translate reality into terms of symbols or images, his ability to think and to imagine. This, particularly in conjunction with the instrument of language, enables him to bring within his mind an increasing range of experience. He does not have to go to a place to know the kind of problems with which he will be faced there, he can think of them, he can create them in his own mind. This 'experiment in ideas' offers a tremendous economy in time because it enables him to take thought for the solution of his problems well in advance of their actually occurring. The highest phase of this internal activity is a process of mental exploration that goes on by means of memories, judgments, perceptions, concepts and ideals derived from previous experience. Thus a man can anticipate the expectations of others and can shape his behaviour accordingly—in short he can become 'socialized'. He is able to develop a self which he thinks conforms to what others expect of him—he may, of course, be wrong in this but at least he has the opportunity of testing out his hypothesis. Thus foresight, planning and anticipation make it possible for a man to create his environment to some extent and they also provide him with the means of controlling it.

As he develops purposes and aims, that is to say guides to what he intends shall take place, he is able to take command of the rudimentary drives of his infancy and redirect them to higher satisfactions. The content of his thought has been provided by his own experience of the world in which he lives and his own reflection upon it. We have insisted that an infant, a child and a man, are restrained, persuaded and coerced by the culture in which they are set but as that man is capable of thought he is able to stand above the culture in some measure.

Our cultural surroundings provide us with cues as to how and what we should learn but in addition, they also influence the selection of what we seek to retain after we have learned it. If you refer back to what has been written above concerning the world of the growing infant in terms of which he has to arrange his own conduct, you will see that as he grows up he is taking roles, he is projecting himself into a social situation in which he plays a part. There are three main stages in this progress in role-taking, as it is called. The first begins when the infant makes automatic imitations of those around him, when he tries to respond as far as he can by doing what they are doing, particularly if this gains applause and appreciation. The second stage may be called the play stage in which he becomes able to take a number of parts and even to act the parts of other people dealing with him. By this means he is trying out several different kinds of self, he is experimenting with his ability to present the parts he thinks other people are playing. It is probable that at this stage his interpretations are unorganized, that he has not the consistency of experience to hold together the various roles he has taken in his play. They are separated from one another and perhaps relatively unrelated in his mind. The third stage we may call the game stage which results in a more organized and consistent behaviour where he tries to see the kind of social situation in which he is to be involved, the organized counterpart of the cultural system. He is now wanting to be all things to all men, he can take a number of different roles while being engaged in the same conversation because he can anticipate the expectations of the various people with whom he is dealing and try to respond to them.

This chameleon existence, however, cannot be indefinitely extended. There has to be a simplification of the variety of human roles and an example of this simplification can be seen in what we call national characteristics. A degree of integration takes place which allows for relatively few alternative interpretations. G. H. Mead, as we shall see later, calls this 'the rule of the generalized other'.[2] In a stable society this generalized image is relatively settled and the varieties of interpretation are few because the main roles are well appreciated and understood. But in a heterogeneous and changing society we have a series of generalized others. For instance in a metropolis like London or Chicago with a large number of nationalities, income groups and cultural backgrounds represented, it is very difficult for a person to be able to move comfortably and with assurance from one group to another. The generalized other of Belgravia is very different from that to be found in Soho. In education part of the process of simplification in roles is to be found in tradition and the transformation and reinterpretation of approved personality traits and accepted character types.

In the educational system of a stable society there is general agreement as to what should be learned, how it should be learned and from whom. It becomes largely a process of growing up and learning by doing from your surroundings—for instance this has been the case in the public schools of this country. It is assumed that there is agreement between parents and the teachers as to what should be taught to the boys and girls and that the cultural background of the school is what the parents want for their children, particularly in the case of boarding schools. Parents are prepared to put their education in the hands of the school and approve of the results even if they do not understand them. In other words they give great importance to the role played by the teacher, particularly by the housemaster or housemistress and the headmaster or headmistress. In the secondary modern school the situation is different. The parents may often not understand the cultural background represented by the school and not regard it as particularly valuable for their child. They may submit, because the law demands it, to their son or daughter being schooled up to the leaving age, but their first interest is in how he or she will earn a living. The role of the teacher in the eyes of the parent is very different in such a situation from the role of the public school master in the eyes of that parent. Just as a person in his social relationships has to take up many roles, so we have to recognize that institutions such as schools also take up many roles. Some say that beauty is in the eye of the beholder and certainly many parents know what part they want the school to play, whether it is to prepare their sons to gain a scholarship to the university, to keep them occupied until they leave school, to teach them useful things like the three R's or engineering or how to use their hands, or to lay the foundations of leadership—and so on.

The last word in this chapter on learning should be on the learning process. There are two great 'laws' with which we are all familiar but which it is easy to overlook. The first is the law of exercise with its converse the law of disuse—doing an action successfully makes it easier to do again and this is obviously fundamental to the whole notion of conditioning. There are three sub-laws related to this. The first of these is the law of frequency which shows that the more frequently we do an act the less attention it requires and this is at the basis of the construction of habits. A child being taught to tie his shoes or to write is setting up a number of motor habits which will become embedded in his experience and not thought of. A group of actions can be co-ordinated in this way and become a more complicated habit with the correspondingly greater difficulty in altering it—for instance the generalized habit of untidiness, or the limited efficiency of typing with one finger of each hand, or the 'bad' habits of an unorthodox batsman. The law of frequency is of very great importance in establishing basic habits and routines, an obvious example of which is the 'overlearning' of tables early in the mathematical career of a child.

A special adaptation of the law of frequency we may call the sub-law of *recency*. Frequency over a given period followed by a lull produces a lapse in efficiency, as occurs when we try to take up a foreign language after a period of time when we have not been using it, or, in the painful experiences of an athlete at the beginning of a new season when he gets into training.

If two processes are performed successfully with comparable frequency at different times, the more recently performed will tend to be done the better, and this has obvious importance in schools as elsewhere, showing itself in the necessity for frequent revision and recapitulation. There is, however, another factor which should be mentioned, the factor of *intensity*. It is not sufficient simply to repeat an act or even to repeat it recently. It is possible for us to learn something at one time which, as we say, we shall never forget, the intensity of the emotion being such that the experience has marked itself deeply in our memories.

The second main law is the law of effect and this has to do

73

with what Hull calls reward. A successful action is one by which we have reached the goal we had in mind, with the accompanying feeling of achievement. However, it is quite possible to have goals which seem to be the same but which are in fact different. For instance, when children are learning poetry they may decide that the important thing is to memorize the passage perfectly and to learn it by whatever means make it come most easily. This gains the marks for memorization but probably kills the poetry. Trial and error learning is another such example where we do not see the way to solve our problem but try and hope for the best; if success ensues then we tend to accept that as the best method possible. Or again the child who decides that the important thing to do is to get the answer in his arithmetic problem right, whether he understands how it has been done or not and so he looks up the answer at the back of the book and tries to dress up his method as convincingly as possible. The teacher would say that such a child is getting an effect, but it is the wrong effect.

If the lesson to be learned from these two main laws of exercise and effect may be related to role-taking, it would appear that in school especially it is important for the teacher to understand what the learner has in mind. It is often easy to teach so that the outward appearances which the teacher wants may be exhibited, but it is more important to try to see what the effects are which the learner considers he is achieving by these results. It is quite true that many incentives act together in a classroom situation to encourage the child to work and give of his best, some of them positive encouragement of rewards, approval or praise, others negative incentives of avoiding punishment, criticism and low standing. But one highly esteemed aim for the good teacher is that his pupil should have as a goal and an incentive in his learning, the satisfaction of understanding and the pleasure of mastery of knowledge. These lead on to the excitement of achieving greater mastery. This is a most complicated effect to aim at and it necessitates a subtle and sustained understanding by the teacher of the roles which he and his pupils have to play and the ideal character types upon which they will both be calling for inspiration from time to time, as well as a shrewd assessment of the working of the laws of frequency and effect.[3]

VIII

Inhibition in Learning

DYNAMIC psychologists hold that we must consider the
whole person when we are talking about learning
because it is the whole person who responds and who
builds in new learning to what is already known in his own
experience. Therefore besides any question of general intellectual capacity and the power to establish relationships in thinking which we commonly call intelligence, we have to recognize
that the inner readiness of a person will greatly matter in his
progress. If he is for one reason or another inhibited or frustrated there are many areas of his capacity for action which may
be affected. It is not sufficient therefore simply to think in
terms of techniques of teaching or to analyse the problems to be
understood in logical terms, we have to take into account the
psychological economy of the learner and this means not simply
his intellectual capacities but the pattern of his emotional life
and the pervading influence of his infantile experience.

Before the war in Germany a number of studies were made
of incapacity in one form or another. This was generally known
as *Psychologie des Nicht Könnens* and it was concerned to a considerable degree with the study of frustration. In this sense
frustration represents a subjective state which blocks satisfying
achievement and because of the continuing failure, a cumulative depression ensues and even any potential success which
might have been possible at the beginning becomes more and
more unlikely. The incapacity in performance which is
obvious is really an incapacity in learning and it may be due to
a number of different factors, among them some innate debility
or handicap or possibly a disturbing or disabling influence in
the field of action itself, or thirdly perhaps some disturbance of

the consciousness of the learner, some attitude of mind which prevents effective learning.[1]

To look at these three aspects of incapacity in order, we see that innate incapacity may show itself in some sense failure, like deafness or blindness or intellectual subnormality or a physical handicap like paralysis or deformity. A person suffering from one or other of these handicaps cannot deal with life in the same way as a normal person may. As he is faced with situations in which he sees himself outdone by others he may find himself spurred on to do as much as he possibly can or he may find a sense of inadequacy and failure mounting. The burden of most wise handling of people with such handicaps in these days is to enable them to do as much as they possibly can for themselves but in any case to accustom them to living with their handicap and coming to terms with it instead of feeling a constant state of inadequacy that they are not otherwise than they are.

In cases such as these we can see more clearly perhaps than normally how important it is that the experience of infancy should lead to an attitude of security and acceptance. It is for this reason that increasingly as time passes we have tried to come to terms in our educational system with the opposite demands made by such handicaps. The first demand is that a child so placed should try to do as much for himself as he possibly can, should try to be as normal as may be. The other demand is that the special problems which his condition presents should be dealt with in their own terms. A child who is blind cannot be taught in the same way as one who sees, one who is deaf has to learn without the use of one of the most important senses of all, an intellectually subnormal child cannot be expected to reach an average school performance, and there are techniques of teaching appropriate to each of these conditions. Yet while we recognize blatant incapacity of this kind and try to deal with it accordingly, there is a wide range of near-incapacity for which we do not always take such care. It is for this reason that in our schools we have to try to keep as flexible a timetable as possible, that we need to have groups small enough to detect what each child can manage. Conversely it is also true to say that children who may in fact have the same sort of difficulties respond to their handicaps very differently and one child of low mental ability may through effort and perseverance reach a higher level of understanding than another; one child who is a very mediocre athlete may wish to succeed with far greater insistence than another. For realistic reasons of administration we very often have to treat wide inequalities as falling within the band of normal distribution and teach children in classes where the range of intelligence varies considerably. Indeed the stigma of abnormality of whatever kind compels some children to try to achieve normality to a stage beyond their capacity.

The second disturbing or incapacitating influence mentioned above was in the field of action; for instance in times of hardship poverty or unemployment is a severe handicap over which the worker has virtually no control. While it is true that exceptional people manage to achieve remarkable things while hungry or homeless or cold, these are the kinds of conditions which sap the energy and achievement of ordinary people. The history of civilizations shows that for any lasting cultural achievement a nation, no less than an individual, has to be assured of the physical necessities of life. The world's culture has not been built during times of war and famine.

To choose a less dramatic situation, children coming from a home which has sapped their confidence or has had a poverty-stricken cultural background, very often find themselves unable to deal with new situations and new opportunities. Shyness, lack of self-confidence and even shame and self-reproach hold a distorting mirror up to their life situations. They do not see the chances which are offered and they are not able to accept themselves or others with confidence. This leads us to the third of the incapacities mentioned above, the disturbance of consciousness concerning the field of action, or as the German word has it *Spielraumbewusstsein*.

We mentioned above the psychological consequences that flow from bad conditions. Alfred Adler based much of his psychology of personality upon the theory of what he called organ inferiority, by which he meant the tendency to inherit organic weaknesses in various parts of the body. Let us suppose that a person begins life with a weak respiratory apparatus and later on suffers, therefore, from speech difficulties. His family as a consequence are likely to seek to correct his speaking and to emphasize the weakness of which he is quite well aware. He feels that he is not being properly understood and that he cannot communicate sufficiently and so he has to give over-attention to this part of his behaviour. This concentration Adler calls compensation and he believes that much of our behaviour is based upon the desire to compensate for inferiority, the conscious or unconscious protest against inadequacy. To him the life-style is established relatively early as a result of the interaction of organic inferiority and the social life which we live as infants. The inferiority sense, which is now a common conversational gambit rather than a technical psychological term, is an example of the interaction of physical and psychological factors. It leads to a chronic distortion of all situations in which the person is involved and to a compensatory form of behaviour which perpetuates the distortion and probably increases it.[2]

While there is obviously a good deal in the personality theory of Adler based upon a sense of inadequacy as a motivation for behaviour, it is different from the dynamic psychology of Freud with its emphasis on aggression and sexuality as the two main instincts. Nevertheless, both men have emphasized the primary importance of the years of infancy in establishing the attitudes and forms of behaviour which reappear in adult life. If this early experience is damaging there is more likelihood of inhibitions arising later which distort our understanding of the situations in which we are placed and our ability to learn. Part of the responsibility of parents and teachers is to see how the inhibitions may be related to a continuing outlook which needs to be counteracted and corrected.

Once it is admitted that frustrations of the learning processes are a part of the frustrations of the whole personality and not simply some problem associated with intellectual functioning a number of things may be said about the dysfunction of the personality as a whole. It is obvious that many cases of educational subnormality are due to organic defect, to some sort of physical deficiency, perhaps caused through illness during pregnancy. Yet there are other forms of mental backwardness which would seem to have a psychological source for the most part. Sometimes a blank failure to understand is related to the effect that the knowledge might have on personal equilibrium. We do not want to understand where it might cause anxiety or guilt or further disturbance of an already precariously balanced personality.

Psychoanalysts maintain that the personality develops out of the control and direction of energies which the infant experiences as associated with its erogenous zones. They consider that if an infant moves without noticeable repression or frustration through the periods of concentrated experience associated with the mouth, the anus and the genitals, the resultant freedom from a sense of guilt and prohibition will show itself in the kind of person that child will become. They consider that if sex curiosity is blocked in infancy and childhood the experience that certain knowledge is tabu may spread to other spheres too. The general curiosity of the child may undergo a stultification and his readiness to enquire for himself may be replaced by a tendency to obey the commands of others. Fenichel says that willingness to find out for ourselves is characteristic of a personality with some self-assurance and confidence and that very often a child who has experienced a veto on knowledge of one kind or another at an early age, is likely to become the sort of person who is prepared to rely on information, upon more and more facts, rather than to indulge in thinking and mental exploration. Religion and politics have often been other areas in which there has been a veto on individual exploration. Both Freud and Adler in different ways drew attention to the fact as they saw it that girls were sometimes unable to accept their femininity and so underwent conflicts within themselves which interfered with their intellectual development.[3]

Schonell and Burt have both conducted very well known and highly accredited investigations into backwardness in school performance. There are three main factors which produce this defective performance. The first environmental, the second intellectual and the third emotional. The environmental factors are such as we would expect and have already mentioned in some measure—poor home conditions and therefore an impoverished home atmosphere; the limitation of out-of-school experiences, crowded classes, absence from school, poor apparatus, understaffed schools and poor teaching. We need not elaborate on these any further because they are thoroughly familiar, unfortunately. The intellectual factors also have to be admitted from the start in those cases to which they apply—the child of poor parental stock and low intellectual ability, mental confusion arising from bad habits of work or poor teaching and the attempt to force a child to achieve a standard beyond its capacity. Both Schonell and Burt[4] agree that very few cases of backwardness can be traced to one cause. They found, as might be expected, that backwardness had many causes or if there was one which predominated it created other problems which aggravated the condition. This was particularly true of the emotional factors which intensified backwardness. These appeared in various attitudes like apathy, a sense of despondency and failure, a loss of confidence and grip and similarly a loss of initiative.

Where there was backwardness in one subject (for instance, arithmetic) the failure here could very often spread to the mental attitudes which lay behind other subjects. While it was quite true that with certain children who had some assurance, the backwardness in one subject might be counteracted by some relative success in others, yet in many cases the sense of failure spread and they found, as Freud and Adler had already indicated, that children began to seek compensatory forms of behaviour which might provide excitement, interest and achievement, and which at the same time would attract the attention of others and give the children concerned some sense of significance. Of course some of these activities are antisocial and Schonell points out that in the case of two thousand delinquents who were seen at a London Child Guidance Clinic, 55 per cent. of them were markedly backward in reading and spelling. Equally he points out, as does Burt, that sympathetic consideration of a pupil's scholastic problems is very often followed by distinct improvement in his behaviour and social adjustment and in his attitude towards his fellows and his teachers. In other words it is to be expected that if we had less backwardness in school we should probably have less maladjustment and in all probability less delinquency.

About a third of the children whom Schonell dealt with who were backward in their spelling, showed some abnormal development of their self-regarding sentiments. These he put into two classes representing extreme aspects. The first were those who on account of repeated failure and wrong treatment had developed what we might loosely term an inferiority sense. Second there were those who developed a compensatory attitude of bluff to hide their shortcomings and who in consequence very often refused to realize or admit their weakness. He quotes one boy who was successful in sport and looked up to by the smaller boys in his class; his arithmetic was good and so he went to a higher class each day for that subject but he was very seriously retarded in spelling and reading. He refused to acknowledge his extreme backwardness endeavouring to convince himself and his schoolmates and even his teacher that he could spell and read as well as anyone in the class. He would hurry through a piece, glibly guessing and extemporizing in an undertone to give the listeners the idea that he knew all the words. Similarly in composition, what he lacked in quality and accuracy he made up for in quantity, and in vocabulary, instead of admitting that he did not know some of the words he was asked to define, he confidently gave meanings for all of them.

To carry out any effective remedial work with such a boy Schonell rightly points out that it was necessary to make him realize that he was cheating himself. The emotional effort to keep up appearances in front of the others was great and in its turn had set up an habitual response—he could not stop from continuing to act the role he had set for himself until he was taken right out of that context.

We see in such a case an example of many of the psychological features which we have been considering in the last chapter on learning and under the heading of this present chapter inhibitions in learning.

Another kind of inhibition appears in some of the forms of passivity with which most teachers are familiar. These represent a resistance to learning and they may have many origins. For instance where intellectual values are rooted in strong identification with parents, a student may encounter a serious conflict when his school or university teaching exposes him to points of view at variance with those which he knows to be valued by his parents, and in some cases this conflict results in a passivity or withdrawal from work. Or again if a student is accustomed to praise or approval for work done and finds in the more casual and independent forms of teaching at the university no such encouragement, he may decide not to make any effort at all. It is certainly true that what is generally called laziness should not be considered as a straightforward irresponsibility and fecklessness on the part of the pupil. It can be a form of escape or a form of resistance which in the same way as confusion and puzzlement deserves to be understood.

If we bring to bear the method of approach which is implicit in what has been said about the psychology of learning, we find that in the case of pupils who seem passive or unwilling to make much effort there are a number of possibilities which we must explore. First of all, is this attitude based upon a record of failure in school work in the past and if so, is this failure partly due to a lack of general ability, a lack of proper groundwork in the subject, too intensive competition with abler pupils at an earlier stage, bad teaching or continued absence from school at a critical period in the development of the subject? Such enquiries as these are necessary in order to understand the intellectual background to the problem. But there are other enquiries which have to be made, too. Is this passivity apparent in all school subjects or are there some where evidence of initiative and enthusiasm are to be found? It may be that the passive behaviour has emotional roots in the treatment that the pupil has experienced from a teacher of this subject earlier on and there has been a transference of the rejection of the teacher to the subject which he taught. The emotional bond may not be with a teacher so much as with the family or the attitude of parents and brothers and sisters to the school or the particular subject.

The important thing that is being stressed here is a deeper interpretation than usual of the cliché about teaching Johnny Latin. The subject that is taught in school is not simply data which the learner has to acquire. From the learner's point of view it is also a symbol which relates him to his teacher. It carries with it strong emotional associations with other teachers and with the family. It is a truism to say that teaching is very different from learning but it is of the greatest importance that we should recognize that the teacher and the learner carry with them their own life-styles and that the subject matter which passes from one to the other is more than acts linking intellect to intellect.

Important as associationist theory is in understanding the learning process and in attempting to offer a descriptive system, it seems only of limited use in educational psychology because the relationship between the teacher and his pupils involves the personality of each. As we have seen in addition, besides this personal relationship there are the roles to be played by each, both pupil and teacher, which give to and maintain in the relationship a certain structure. I would maintain that a dynamic psychology can give a much fuller account of what takes place than can associationist psychology.[5] Moreover, I consider that psychoanalysis, while being helpful to the understanding of the pupil-teacher relationship is incomplete unless it is given a social context. While this is especially true for education it is of course also true in any attempt to give an account of personality.

In this book it has been necessary to establish after the theoretical background of the first part, a psychological structure developing from it. Now we are at the stage where we must turn to the social aspects of personality development.

PART THREE

SOCIAL ASPECTS OF
PERSONALITY DEVELOPMENT

IX

The Social and Cultural Concept of Personality

MANY of our concepts of personality are based upon Platonic notions of the existence of the soul. According to these principles man lives on two levels. There is the principle of truth which is in the universe itself and man at his best is able to apprehend this idea and form of truth compared with which his individual experiences are like bubbles on the surface of a flowing stream. Nevertheless it is his daily experience which forms the second level of man's existence and Plato in the seventh book of *The Republic* describes in the allegory of the Cave the different responses which men can make to the world in which they live. Only very few among men, those who are equipped to become the philosopher-kings, are willing and able to venture into the light of things as they are and to turn away from the shadows with which they have formerly been living. The shadows are the symbols of daily experience and the light of things as they are outside the cave represents the Form of the Good.[1]

Christian doctrine has also the notion of man as a being who is a stranger here because heaven is his home. There are many important differences between the Christian and the Platonic view of man but they have this in common, that each of them believes man to be unique and possessed of a supra-temporal soul. For the Christian, justice represents the most equitable form of controlling man's behaviour in time, and righteousness represents the quality of behaviour which has its justification beyond time. Everyone, according to the Christian, is made in this mould and has a destiny beyond history. According to such a doctrine, therefore, while man is set in time and a culture, he is also able to share in some measure in eternity and the Christian theory of selfhood has to take into account these two dimensions of human experience.

G. H. Mead, Linton, Kardiner and Dewey[2] are representatives of a theory of personality which takes into account only the interaction between man and his environment. Theirs is a naturalistic and not a supernatural interpretation of the nature of self and the meaning of personality. For Dewey the personality exists in its environment not as coins are in a box but as a plant is in sunlight and soil. Moral control to him arises from knowledge gained through the experience of living and what is proved and workable. Conscience can be accounted for in naturalistic terms and does not need to have the Christian or Platonic appeal to supernatural origins.

According to the theory of social interaction of G. H. Mead a child does not possess a self at birth. Its early behaviour is diffuse and may be interpreted in terms of cycles of activity. The infant has to learn what he can do and how he can do it from the response which others give to him or by the satisfaction which he experiences within himself. At this very early stage in his life and for quite a long while afterwards there is little self-awareness and certainly no self-observation. His behaviour flows out from him to others in a desire for immediate satisfaction of his rudimentary needs. He begins to show signs of becoming aware of others when he includes in his actions some anticipation of their response and so controls and directs his actions accordingly, using his lips, his tongue and his hands and, as time passes, signs of recognition and smiles. In other words he is learning to control and direct his behaviour in terms of what others expect of him.

This is a simple illustration of an important principle in Mead's theory of the emergence of the self. He says that the sense of identity emerges not out of action by the person but out of interaction after one has perceived other people and established some sense of relationship with them and some idea of how our actions or behaviour is called out, our ability to do something in response to them. Only when this sense of being able to initiate action is present can we say that there are the beginnings of selfhood and the kind of action which is initiated must arise out of a choice of possible actions or else it would seem to be determined and no question of choice or initiation would arise. Selfhood is only possible therefore when the infant has had a sufficiently long independent existence to accumulate experience.

This notion Mead develops into his theory of role-taking which is a more protracted and organized form of response by the infant to what is expected of him. He comes to know the sound of his mother's words, tones, bodily movements and gestures as she deals with his wishes and wants and ultimately the infant takes into his own experience, or introjects as the psychoanalysts say, what his mother does. He begins to understand something of the whole picture of interaction between himself and his mother and he begins to assume what Mead calls an organized role in which he plays his part because he knows the part which his mother is going to play. From that kind of experience grows his ability to see himself as an object and in time he has some interest in trying to see himself as others do.

An interesting and rather difficult point of interpretation arises here. Very often children in their second or third year express their wants in sentences such as the following: 'Jimmy wants this,' 'Susan likes that' and some psychologists have interpreted this as an ability in the child to talk to himself as others have talked to him and so to provide himself with what Cooley calls 'his looking-glass self'.[3] The difficulty of interpretation arises in the way in which the child has learned about himself. The personal pronoun 'I' comes into his vocabulary after he has known and used his own given name. All his experience hitherto has been of hearing himself talked to as Jimmy and naturally this is the sound which he will associate with himself. All the pronouns are shorthand versions of proper names and can only be used when a certain degree of linguistic sophistication has been achieved. It can be a matter of some difficulty for a child to appreciate that 'Susan' and 'I' represent the same person.

Nevertheless having pointed out this difficulty I would go on to say that children do talk to themselves and do provide themselves with many different parts in the dramas which they create and in which they are the sole performers. In overhearing the child at play in this way, taking first one part and then another and including himself as only one of the actors, we can get some idea of the scope of a child's comprehension, we can see with what degree of accuracy and complexity he places himself in relation to other people and to things. We have often watched young children playing the role of mother, providing themselves with pots and pans either in reality or in imagination and going about their daily business with other members of the family in terms of make-believe. They can be nurse, fireman, soldier, shopkeeper, customer, schoolchild—they can experiment in this way with many different roles and become aware, at any rate in theory, of how other people might act or behave. Many writers on young children have emphasized the range and flexibility of their dramatic play.

Young children play more or less individually. The actions of others interfere in their play space and even when two or more children in the first three or four years of life seem to be playing together, they are very often pursuing separate stories and doing different things. They have an ability to insulate themselves from one another and maintain their own fantasy-world, calling upon others here and there. Round about seven or eight years of age we find much more readiness to play games in which others are involved, even to the extent of choosing sides and making up teams. Usually these games are not much formalized into rules and it is not easy for young children of this age to maintain the framework of the formal team game which we come upon later. Nevertheless it is important that the membership of a group or a team is so often a part of play at this stage. We see it in the collective rushing about of boys or girls, their frequently ruthless exclusiveness and the degree of individual imitative and dramatic skill.

Piaget in *The Language and Thought of the Child*[4] makes a distinction between what he calls egocentric and socialized speech. Egocentric speech involves no attempt to interchange ideas or to see another person's point of view. It is what Piaget calls a 'collective monologue' or a 'pseudo-conversation'. On the other hand socialized speech reveals the talker really speaking to a listener, considering his possible replies, making an attempt to communicate ideas and make himself understood. According to Piaget, children think and act more egocentrically up to the age of seven or thereabouts and despite their apparent interplay of ideas at an earlier age, they are not usually considering one another's viewpoint. He considers that children below the age of seven or eight for the most part have not the intellectual equipment to understand points of view other than their own. Even their own private thoughts are not open to very much personal analysis in the sense that few children, he says, check their own private thinking and conclusions in the way in which an older child or adult tries to see what he has to say in the context of other people's points of view.

Susan Isaacs and others have challenged Piaget's viewpoint in detail and consider that some of the data which he offers are not representative of children in other contexts. Isaacs and the others claim that children are capable of behaving in a self-consciously social fashion at a much earlier age, say at three or four.[5] However, even though the weight of available evidence may run counter to Piaget's rather clean-cut differentiations, there is a much greater degree of egocentric language and outlook in children before school age than after and certainly this is in line with the social development of young children which Piaget has also considered.

At the ages of nine and ten and on to puberty, we find the role of the child takes into account much more what others expect of him. He is developing his social self and we can see this happening in the change which takes place in the games that he plays. Now he starts on team games proper—football, hockey and the like. And here in order to play his own part he has to understand what the parts played by others in the team are. The framework of control which the rules of the game represent is now much better understood and it is possible for children in this stage of their development to have a sense of strategy. It is in this phase also that we find very often the beginnings of gang behaviour, sometimes with a considerable degree of ritual and self-submergence to a code. When he becomes involved in this way, when he both participates in what has been done by a group and at the same time bears a responsibility for some part of this action, then the child is beginning to experience the reciprocal behaviour which lies at the basis of role-taking.

Just as in learning we develop concepts out of many concrete and specific experiences which we call perceptions, so we develop general attitudes and ideas out of a wide variety of different roles. In infancy we develop the notion of our selfhood *vis-à-vis* our parents, our brothers and sisters, the family circle, friends and acquaintances, and later we have to come into contact with institutions more directly.

The first and most obvious of these is the school and many of the roles which we can play in childhood arise out of this situation in which we are under a certain amount of compulsion and in the control of an adult and we pursue a curriculum as a common concern with other children of our own age. The play group, the church, the mass media of information and entertainment, later the voluntary bodies like scouts and guides— these are the institutions within which we begin to see ourselves, not only in relation to other children and other adults, but also in relation to codes of behaviour expected of us, ideals to be pursued, behaviour which is *de rigueur*.

Social maturity and responsibility depend on being able to take part in a number of human relationships while at the same time distilling out from these a certain generalized consistency and continuity of the kind of part which we want to play, the kind of person we want to be. A young child has very little character development in the sense in which that term is usually understood, because he has not yet had time to build up what G. H. Mead calls a 'generalized other' or 'integrated role', which is worked out in terms of the moral expectations of the community and the individual choice of the child as he begins to realize his own responsibility in each situation.

Marx as well as Jung spoke about the masks which we assume and impose upon our self-assertiveness. Man unfolds his abilities only by virtue of the social relationships in which he is called upon to act and the character masks he comes to assume. Perhaps it should be said that a mask in the sense in which we are here using it is not meant to imply some form of concealment of another and less desirable self. We very often assume a mask to be a form of disguise, but in this sense it is being used more as a means of expression which is called out of the actor in the situation by what he feels ready and able to do with his knowledge of the people with whom he is dealing and what is expected of him. Mead tries to solve this difficult problem by considering the self under two headings, 'I' and 'me'. He says that the self is not so much a substance as a process in which a conversation between the 'I' and the 'me' takes place as it were.

The 'me' is the more or less integrated set of attitudes and ideas of other people which we have built together as our conscious experience from which we choose roles to represent our own ideas of ourselves. Many of these are roles which we know the community has come to expect us to perform. The 'I' is the self as actor or initiator, the agent of change. Moreno speaks of the 'I' as self-propelling activity and it is in the domain of the 'I' that we find the notion of responsibility, the uniqueness and coherence and waywardness of choice. Without the 'I' there could not be a notion of responsibility nor could there be an expectation of novelty or unexpectedness in experience. While different aspects of 'me' depend upon my social and cultural training and the particular configurations of time and place, the 'I' represents the sense of self-identity in the possessor of the experiences.[6]

One important factor in identification of various kinds of 'me' is the process which we might call the acquisition of status. As we grow up we assimilate the status values which others accord to us and we begin to accord to them. Self-esteem emerges as a self-regarding attitude in which our standing is reflected in the opinions which others seem to have of us. Self-esteem becomes a very important centre of motivation and indeed of the organization of life, because it is the area of our self where inner and outer controls meet. The status implies a hierarchy of preference and while it is true that as infants we tend to identify with the roles which our parents expect of us, as our experience grows and we become aware of a variety of roles, we also become aware of a preference for one role, expected by those whom we love and respect, while we ourselves may have a wish to play another. Very often a sense of guilt or disapproval becomes attached to one role and approval to another.

As time passes we internalize this set of preferences and begin to work out consciously and unconsciously a scale of aspiration. What a child or a man sets out to accomplish will reflect fairly well what those around him want to achieve and usually in our kind of competitive society the aspiration level which parents have for their children and which adults have for themselves, may be at some distance from the present achievement level. This is very obviously the case in relation to the ambitions for a career. A young man or woman has to make his way in a world where those possessing knowledge and experience have already preceded him and achieved the level to which he aspires.

A society manipulates the degree of distance which there is between achievement level and aspiration level and it also helps to give content to the goals to be aimed at. In our culture I think it would be true to say that there is an emphasis on the notion of success defined in material terms. Material wealth is usually desired, though the degree of affluence varies very widely. Similarly we have a stress upon individual achievement and much less on shared achievement. Competition is one of the means which is highly valued in our western civilization and co-operation is much less evident, at any rate in the industrial and commercial sectors of life. This statement is much less true in farming communities, where we find more co-operative attitudes, at any rate in the big issues of survival and the struggle against the elements.

William James pointed out that a man's social self was made up of the recognition which he got from his mates. We are not only gregarious animals who like to be near to our fellows, we are also self-assertive and we seem to have a deep-set desire to have ourselves noticed and particularly to be noticed favourably and approvingly.[7] James pointed out that properly speaking a man has as many social selves as there are individuals who recognize him and carry an image of him in their minds.

The value of Mead's approach is that he underlines for us that the self is not given but emerges out of our social experience. Responsibility is not a quality with which we are born but emerges out of the chances we have had to learn, according to our degree of maturity, how to act responsibly, so that as time has passed we have been able to develop a concept of what it means.[8]

This analysis is quite in keeping with the great educational traditions in the Anglo-Saxon countries where there has been for some time an emphasis on the values of character training through both intellectual and social experience. For instance, the boarding school is an obvious institution for the development of a strategy of teaching responsibility through social action to children. There is a significant difference between the British approach to education here and the Continental method where a much greater emphasis has been placed on the primary importance of books and intellectual achievement. Also associated in the past with the British boarding school tradition has been a tendency to preach and sermonize by which it was hoped that by direct instruction, precept and example, a desirable pattern for a generalized 'me' would be held up for emulation by the pupils. Mead and Dewey would say that while this obviously has a place, a more effective form of teaching of this kind can be found in the community life relationships of people, because we do not acquire these attributes by taking thought, or even one by one as they are understood intellectually. The task of the educator is to plan learning so that responsibility is being understood through action and through accepting the role which you know others expect you to play. There is an obvious place here for sport and out-of-school activities of all kinds, such as has been advocated for many generations, at any rate in the public and grammar schools of England, and it is interesting to see that youth training is based on the same principles. By these means the aspiration levels in different activities can always be raised and so the kind of aspiration proper to the idealized 'me' can extend in range and moral quality.

Hartshorne and May in their studies of deceit showed that moral traits, such as honesty, truthfulness, faithfulness, are not necessarily unified qualities in character, always expressing themselves in virtuous behaviour in whatever context. According to them people who would be ranked high on their moral qualities behave with a different degree of moral rectitude in different situations. They declare that there is no automatic carry-over from one situation to another and that religious ideals are no guarantee of generalized virtue. A man who is honest in his business dealings, who is an upright husband, faithful to his wife, or at any rate seldom unfaithful, may not be a reliable tax payer.[9]

While there has been a great deal of further research done in this field on the tendency for ideals to extend over a wide area of behaviour and some of it has a more favourable story

8   95

to tell, nevertheless, the main point of the investigations of Hartshorne and May still stands. They say that children are likely to respond better to situations from which they can learn how to behave and what to do than they are to the statements of those in authority. Obviously in life and in educational process, children and adults learn in both ways but the moral of what Hartshorne and May suggest is that from the point of view of successful education, it is better to arrange the situations so that the children may teach themselves through the social ways which they take up than that they should accept primarily what has been laid down as example or precept from those in authority. There is no great originality in a statement of this kind baldly presented, but if we translate it into terms of educational practice we may very often find that we are relying more upon 'do as I say' than upon 'do as I do' or even 'find out for yourself what you should do in this situation'.[10]

When we talk about role-taking as an educational method we have in mind that group activities can help to build up within the framework of the group incentives, rewards, motives, instruments of analysis. The mutual control in such a situation arises because the sense of responsibility and of conscience is anchored in the ways in which the children in the group behave to one another and the expectations that they have of one another. Moreno suggests that it is more desirable to think of the role as a point of reference, than the personality or the ego, because these are less concrete and, as he says, wrapped up in 'metapsychological mysteriousness'.

If educators are concerned with the development of the self the concepts of 'me' and 'I' can be of considerable help to them because it is the living act which brings about a fusion of these two aspects of selfhood. The act of choosing and the action itself never get directly into experience in their full quality until after the act has taken place and then only with difficulty. What happens then is that we catch it in our memory and we place it in terms of what has been done. The decision to act and the action in its various forms together form part of the 'I'. Yet there is something further and equally elusive about this concept, this continuing self. It is the notion of identity and continuity of self awareness. Not only is one aware of oneself as someone who has done actions in the past

96

and has therefore acquired an experience, one is aware that one will continue to act in unforeseeable ways and this sense of the past, the present and the future, caught up in self-identification is a notion of the greatest value to the Platonist, the Christian, the idealist and to the social psychologist. But there are certain features of Mead's analysis which do not usually appear in the thinking of the idealist.

To the idealist the growth of moral personality consists in the individual development of each person, in the improvement of the powers of the self and the sharpening of reasoning capacity. Similarly he is concerned with the removing of prejudices because these represent a fixed and limited response to new moral dilemmas. The idealist is concerned with sensitive and informed response by each person, but he has little to say about the method. At such a time he moves from his philosophic position to ask himself psychological questions.

A sociological theory of the self such as that held by G. H. Mead does not start off with a philosophic position like the idealist's. Mead's first contention is that the self is not a metaphysical entity, it is a process of behaviour and response realized in time. It is not innate or given from birth, it is built up from experience and it gains its definition in response to and in opposition to the social process in which it is set. Man has the unique psychological endowment to enable him to become self-conscious but the form which that self-consciousness will take, the context of the personality, only the external field in which he lives can provide. Mead goes so far as to say, 'mind is nothing but the social importation of the external process into the conduct of the individual so as to meet the problems which arise'.

It might appear that Mead side-steps the question of the nature of the uniqueness of man's position. At any rate Mead's eye is fixed upon man as he grows in this society with the psychological equipment that he has. The 'I' as the continuing self might be considered to be an enigmatic concept but Mead wishes simply to recognize the self-regulating and unifying function of this aspect of our experience. Theoretically it would be possible for an idealist to accept Mead's kind of analysis of the self whilst keeping his reservations about the meaning of this enigmatic 'I'.

97

Moreno makes a distinction somewhat similar to Mead's when he speaks of the 'content self' and the 'act self'. So many of our creations place a premium on memory and our ability to conserve and preserve the culture of the past. For instance, our reliance upon the printed word, the film, the recording, enable us to make contact with a past spontaneity, a past experience, but also they tend to make us live life at one remove. Our labour-saving devices which are supposed to open new opportunities to us because of the time and energy saved present us with the possibility of promoting leisure which leads to inertia. While there is an immense advantage in being able to make a detailed reliable and lively contact with the past, our daily life in an urbanized society does not face us with sufficient experience of living in the present and preparing for the future. It may mean that while we are much better informed than our forebears we have become far less self-reliant and self-sufficient. The attitude of mind inevitable in these days is that no single person can know more than a tiny fragment of the quantum of human experience and that inevitably there is a huge area of knowledge which is known by other minds but which will never be communicated to any one person. The result is a potentially paralysing awareness that all judgment and activity are partial and that we rely upon the machines we have created to give us the information which we want. Moreno puts it dramatically when he says that the spontaneity of human beings is threatened by the robots and the technical animals which man has created.

The result of all this is a curious contradiction in our contemporary dilemma. We create more and more machines with confidence, we find a hundred different ways of working more efficiently and faster and in that sense we change and advance but we have no confidence that we know what to do with the time and the opportunity which these creations of ours offer to us. On the one hand, therefore, we go forward into the future with an ostensible confidence and reliance on our ingenuity; on the other we have a chronic sense of insufficiency because we feel aware of a race between the momentum of invention on the one side and the precarious mastery of self-annihilation on the other.

Moreno reasserts that man is a creator and he claims that

education above all must take its stand on this belief and just shape what it does according to this principle. Otto Rank in a monograph first published in 1941 privately by friends and students of the author, takes up the same theme. Man is an original and an originator and no one can live another person's life for him. A teacher may have a pupil who is known to be above average in his abilities but the teacher cannot decide whether this child is to become a genius, a fool or an outcast. Only the child's response to living itself, only his readiness to take chances and realize his potentialities can answer this question. No amount of psychological experimentation and controlled tests can do so. In this sense Rank is thinking of help which one human being can give to another, not of a planned method of psychotherapy. Each of us has to experience the irrational forces within himself which in the normal outlook on education are usually ignored or overlooked. In this way Rank declares himself an opponent of the school of psychological engineering of Watson, Hull and Skinner. At the same time he is at pains to point out that this conception does not mean giving free range to the hidden desires of the ego but rather permits the individual to accept his own inner limitations, his psychological endowment or the outer restrictions that he perceives around him, on his own terms, with free volition. Rank believes that Freud's psychoanalysis offered a conceptual framework which was too deterministic to leave room for any constructive development of self autonomy and responsibility. He says that it is quite possible that a causal framework like Freud's offers an explanation of compulsive or neurotic attitudes and behaviour, but it cannot account for the initiative of healthy creativeness. Accordingly, for Rank, the aim of therapy and of education cannot be told in terms of adjustment which is a passive and manipulative concept. It has to be told in terms of autonomy in the individual, the liberation and realization of his potentialities.[10]

X

Creative Education

IN common with the dynamic psychologists I believe that there is in everybody a psychological energy which seeks to express itself in satisfying experience. We can emphasize spontaneity as Rank does, or we can stress conditioning and control. In our daily life as might be expected and in educational practice we tend to move from one to the other. Rank makes the point that control comes from a creative effort as much as from submission to external conditions. He says that the will is the united and balancing force in human behaviour, having a two-fold function, being at one time an impulsive and at another an inhibiting force. So we have the paradox that the will can manifest itself in free self-expression or in self-imposed inhibition arising out of acceptance of control from things as they are. The ideal to be aimed at is an ability to accept oneself not with resignation, but with a sense of achievement, in which aspiration is not a stultifying perfection but a satisfying incentive which keeps achievement and ambition in creative tension.

When we speak of creative behaviour very often we imply highly unusual and original achievements. This is not at all what I have in mind in this chapter. While I could illustrate what I mean through choosing an example from a child studying arithmetic or geography, let me illustrate the point from the study of music, because very often for many people music has about it a mystique which confuses argument.

Really, music is not primarily an art, it is a form of expressing in a special kind of sound feelings which we as individuals want to put into some kind of action. However, in our society we have turned it into something objective which has rules, conventions and a status of social and intellectual standing.

Quite often we talk about music as an art form with a system of notation which needs study and technical mastery. We think of music as the work of the composer and the performer, we think of it as experience written down in musical form in order to be reproduced when the notation has been understood. This is the aspect of music which Moreno calls cultural conservation.

Let me not be misunderstood. I am not for a moment suggesting that it is not perfectly proper that we should have developed music in this way. Obviously art represents a disciplining of native impulse into a refinement of form, but for many people music, like the other arts, is created and performed by people with special gifts. It is associated with high technical excellence and with creative originality; it is essentially the province of the composer, the conductor, the singer and the instrumentalist. In this view music is not what happens to us when we are setting free our own energies in sound or song.

In these days of dissemination to the masses through high-grade reproduction of excellent performances we are creating a greater general knowledge of music and at the same time a wider gap between what we have become accustomed to hear and what we can ourselves achieve. It is true of course that we obtain a vicarious emotional experience through hearing some of the world's great music played by great orchestras but the very excellence of the performance may prevent many people from venturing on their own self-realization through music. We still tend to think of music as being composed by some specially gifted people which the rank and file of the rest of us can reproduce up to a point and which a very small minority of us can perform really well. Music as spontaneous creation for most of us in the western world never becomes a possibility. Nevertheless, in our schools in these days we are encouraging young children to sing and play in their own way and this is all to the good, for while music is an art form, at a more rudimentary level it can be spontaneous sound.

We can see the flow of dynamic energy being channelled into socially desirable forms most clearly in infancy. Children learn to speak, walk, draw, write and count. In fantasy and in play they bring their private worlds and the demands of time, space and society closer together. The ways in which a child has learned to inhibit and canalize his spontaneous energy are of the greatest importance to any understanding of creative education. It is probable that every attempt at doing something has in most cases an antecedent vision of the act which is to be performed and as the child's imaginative power develops, so the range of his fantasy world grows. The main task of the adult is as far as possible not to hamper the opportunities for expression in movement, in speaking, in singing, touching, tasting, and not to expect too early a self-consciousness to enter into spontaneous action. We should not want the child too early to reflect upon the relationships between his private world and the world as we know it. The maxim of the parent and the educator should rather be 'let it happen' than 'make him do this or that'—let the child pick up the language and do not urge him to do it. Encouragement in the early years is of inestimable importance for the development of confidence and spontaneity later on. Too often correcting, denying, belittling, forbidding, lead to diffidence later. In most cases slowness or difficulty connected with walking, talking or physical development are overcome under the pressure of ordinary living. The anxieties of parents who begin to wonder if their child lacks some kind of innate qualities beget tension in the family circle.[1]

One of the unsought-for advantages of regarding music and the arts as attainments open in adult life to the very few, is that we do not expect in young children any very great technical success in either of these fields of activity. While it is obviously true that with our present knowledge of physical development in children we know that their voices and their muscle development are not sufficiently advanced to permit technical excellence early in life, there is not the pressure to expect it in the arts such as exists, for instance, in the case of counting, speaking and writing. So in the arts the pressure of standards does not enter so early into a child's experience, there is a longer time for spontaneity. Added to this, in recent years in particular, those responsible for the teaching of the arts have lain great emphasis on the encouragement and support of the spontaneity of children. It is heartening to see that these attitudes are current coin in the theory and practice of teachers of young children.

As we grow older and continue through our school career,

we find that we are asked to pay attention to things we may not wish to consider and to make an effort to understand material which we would prefer to ignore. We cannot expect that pupils will always and in every place want to work at what is put before them, but if we adapt the principle of the output of spontaneous energy we can obtain a great deal of guidance on the attitude of mind which will enjoy grappling with new experience. If we are dealing with an adolescent who is resistant to work in school, we can rely on it that part of his opposition is to be sought for in the inhibitions that have been built up in infancy. It is not idle to think that in some cases children who have obtained a quite unexpected release and achievement in a new subject, such as painting or modelling, have found success where they may very easily have expected to discover once again only failure and boredom. It is for this reason that, as we said earlier when we were discussing inhibition and learning, we should regard the learning process as one which engages the whole personality. While we can recognize competition and the search for status as a sociological phenomenon, the psychological reality of this feature is to be found in the emotional life of persons and nowhere is this more true than in schools. Very few schools or teachers have the courage to believe that the best service to failure in, say, mathematics may be to suspend it for some time and to give the pupil the opportunity to re-establish his self-confidence by discovering success in something else— say art or drama. We ought to think of the curriculum as an instrument by means of which we can help children to spontaneous achievement rather than to the avoidance of failure or even more seriously to the confirmation that poor standards are inevitable.

It should be added for those people who emphasize the need for standards and who consider that success is a matter of effort, and failure is largely due to laziness, that Rank's spontaneity theory also aims at high standards. The difference lies in the attitude of mind of the pupil in attaining those standards. Rank wants the pupil to engage in good work because he can allow his mental energies to flow in that direction with zest—for him the impulse comes from a concentration of psychological effort because there is an absence of conflict. To far too many teachers the only measure to be respected is the examination performance, regardless of what has happened in the psychological economy of the pupil. It has been the experience of very many teachers and psychotherapists that if they can retrace the present failure to its roots in the earlier inhibition or inferiority, it is very often possible to rebuild new learning associated with success because of the spontaneous impulses which each of us possesses.

While it is true that in some cases the personal relationship of psychotherapist and patient is necessary for such rehabilitation, it is obviously unrealistic to expect that this could often be possible, even if it were seen to be the best method of realizing what the problem is and how to treat it. Very often it is far more practicable and successful to work through groups where the sense of unique oddity and failure is reduced and where a mutual sympathy in the members of the group can produce the enveloping trust in which success becomes possible.

Many teachers reject such ideas on the grounds that they are too old to learn such new methods and that many of the children they teach misunderstand an attitude of sympathy and consideration as a sign of weakness. Not only so, but the norms in tough schools incorporate the expectation of a certain amount of violence and authoritarianism. Perhaps the most important thing of all is the recognition that for a teacher to be successful in putting Rank's spontaneity theory into practice he has in the first place to free his own latent energies and to be prepared to dispel much of his own destructiveness, academicism and fear. It will also mean that the teacher has to make a genuine attempt to understand what are the motivations both negative and positive of the children he teaches. He can call upon the curriculum to help him to some extent in this exploration—for instance through the written work which the pupils do it is very often possible to explore what their out-of-school activities are, what kind of things they like and why and what their antipathies are. In social contacts out of school, perhaps at school camps or in casual conversation away from the classroom, we may loosen up the more formal contacts of the teacher and the pupil. Similarly in the arrangement of school government and the distribution of responsibility, further insight may be obtained into the way in which children behave in such circumstances. There is of course the whole field of formal and informal testing—Moreno has developed a valuable instrument in sociometric tests of the inter-relationships between members of a group, and there are in existence forms of personality inventory which could be used in moderation to yield further insight. Achievement in the various subjects of the curriculum can in itself often be helpful in building up a picture of what the child is managing to do when faced with the academic demands of the school and very often how relationships with other teachers are working out.

Just as the written work of a pupil can be used to help a teacher's understanding, so too can his work in art and in drama. Indeed Moreno has developed a technique of socio-drama and psycho-drama as a means of diagnosis and as a possible means of therapy in his whole theory of psychology.[2] I am not suggesting that his techniques may be directly transferred for use with children in school as a part of the curriculum, but I have in mind that the principles on which his methods have been worked out could be adapted with profit to use in school—indeed it has already been used for this kind of purpose. Likewise the subjects chosen in painting and the methods of execution can be of help to the discerning teacher.

D. H. Lawrence in *The Rainbow* and other novelists have painted a convincing picture of the hatred and hostility which can exist in the classroom. A teacher is exposed more than most people to destructive tendencies within his pupils and within himself. It is all the more important, therefore, that he should realize what are the realities of the classroom in terms of the attitudes which his pupils bring with them toward him as a person and as a symbol of authority. Similarly, he must come to terms with the desires in himself to behave resentfully which, by reason of his authority, he can very often get away with. Equally he must give himself the chance of happiness and success in his relationships by discovering within the school the opportunities for spontaneity and creativeness both within himself and within his pupils. Too much repression and supression is a potent source of neurosis. The attitude of authoritative control in education very often produces negativism toward learning itself. A teacher must at some time ask himself, 'Do I rely upon the fact that my pupils must do what I tell them or do I want them to use the knowledge which I present as of value in itself but also as a symbol of the spontaneous growing of the self?' This may seem a rhetorical question but it is not intended as such. Anyone who tried to answer it honestly would have to undergo a ruthless self-examination and he would have to take a steady look at the opportunities for destructive competition and for the avoidance of responsibility which exist in school and in society in general.

It is dismally true that in the minds of many children school remains a daily routine. Seldom for such pupils is there a moment of excitement when they are put into an unexpected situation, whether it be a new and promising problem in the curriculum or the challenge of finding their way across country by compass and map. Indeed, one of the reasons why games are so highly valued, leaving aside the leisure-work dichotomy, is that the result is not known until the end of the game, until the final efforts have been made. Kurt Hahn in his school at Salem and later at Gordonstoun has for many years stressed the importance of individual challenge as perhaps the most important element of all in education.

Creative education comes about when children are active of their own volition whether it be in the simple skills of walking, talking or playing, or in the spontaneous, unstylized achievement of child art, or in physical effort, or in individual intellectual success.

In 1915 John Dewey said, 'At present the tendency is to conceive individual mind as a function of social life, as not capable of operating by itself, but as requiring continuous stimulus from social agencies and finding its nutrition in social supplies'.[3] This tendency is probably more marked than ever in these days and it is of paramount importance in education that we encourage a true sense of individuality and self-awareness. This is an educational aim of value in itself but perhaps of especial importance at present as a means of counter-acting what Dewey outlined. It has been our especial concern in this chapter to draw attention to some of the psychological prerequisites in trying to realize this aim in the present day.

XI

Culture and Personality

THE sociologist is interested to see how the general structure of the self develops from the parts which a man plays consciously and unconsciously in the society and culture to which he belongs. By culture we mean the established and learned ways of doing things, the beliefs, the ideals and the objects and tools which a society uses. For instance in the west we have developed the distinctive muscular habits which come into play when we sit in chairs and we have become accustomed to this from our childhood. In the east they are accustomed to sitting on the floor with the different muscular habits which this entails. We have a routine of eating and sleeping and we even become hungry at culturally determined hours. The English people are supposed to be fond of animals, particularly of dogs, cats and horses and encourage definite emotional attitudes in their children toward these animals. In other countries the cow is sacred and the pig is unclean. For the English child this is a relatively flexible attitude (after all not all English people are fond of animals) but for the Indian or the Jewish child the attitude is really a conviction which is deeply associated with religious belief and practice.

If we turn to the family, we again find patterns of relationships which are accepted from a very early age. We have very often in this book mentioned the importance of the earliest experience that infants have with their mothers and later with their fathers and other members of the family. Freud has made the family triangle situation one of the main axes on which personality structure is based. This attitude to the family shows itself not only in the parent-child relationship, but in the kinship structure as a whole and in the mating conventions which exist. In some civilizations it is customary for marriages to be arranged by parents or relations and not by the young people themselves. In others virginity is highly valued and the girl is protected until she is married. But it is not uncommon to find in some cultures a freedom in premarital sexual relationships and no great expectation that a girl will be a virgin until she is married.

Status relations are another dimension on which many habits of thinking and feeling are built up; we have seen how women were highly valued in the chivalric tradition, and in ancient Chinese culture old people had a standing which was accorded to nobody else. In our own day in this country we have become accustomed to thinking of the two-generation family as being the most desirable form of living but as anthropologists have very often shown, the clan or the tribal family provides a quite different context in which children can grow up.

We are now agreed in the western world that the techniques of nursing and child care represent the earliest form of experience which infants have of the world into which they have come. We have had various fashions concerning the feeding of children; sometimes they have been fed when they seemed to want it and at other times only at regular intervals. In some cultures the mother has been encouraged to make the time of feeding pleasurable both to herself and to her baby and in others the child has been hurried to finish and all demonstrations of affection have been cut short. Sometimes infants have been weaned early and at others they have been fed by their mothers until they were two or even three years of age. With some families and tribes it is customary to treat the children permissively and as valued members of the family and with other groups they are told to be seen and not heard and are made aware of their junior and dependent position, very often by means of punishment of different kinds against which they cannot retaliate.

In every culture means have to be found to deal with conflicts and clashes of interest and these means in their turn help to block or put difficulties in the way of future actions. For instance, the whole system of law is an attempt to establish a principle of equity which indicates that certain kinds of behaviour will attract the recriminations and punishment of the society. The law is intended on the one hand by implication to indicate what kind of behaviour the society values and on the other to provide a means of deterring the anti-social person who does not take the hint.

It is usual also to find in the arrangements which grow up in a culture some means of permissible and legitimate outlet for blocked self-assertiveness. For example, in earlier forms of society these tendencies were able to express themselves fairly directly in warfare, warlike games or hunting and other forms of taxing and risky exercise. Everyone in our day accepts that if we can possibly get rid of warfare we must do this—that is to say that we do not want to have this kind of direct outlet for aggressiveness in the future. We have a number of other ways of trying to make allowances for this tendency, even though for most of us living in cities with shops to supply our need and the whole international economy based on the division of labour and supply and demand, hunting is no longer either necessary or possible. So we have devised team games as a kind of socialized warfare. Competition is the basis of most of these games whether by pitting yourself against others directly, as in the case of a boxing match, an athletics meeting or a tennis competition; or sometimes against a record or a privately held challenge such as we find in the case of a weight-lifter or a mountaineer.

We have already indicated in this book that behaviour itself represents a discharge of psychological energy, an outlet in behaviour. These outlets, this behaviour, has to take some definiteness of form and come to possess some internal coherence before we can consider it to be a culture. As man has the ability to turn in upon his own experience and create a world of fantasy we can have in any culture evidence of his internal world and at the same time of his external achievement both in relation to the things he makes and the means by which he lives in company with his fellows. Accordingly, myth, religion, art forms, legal systems, governments, forms of social approval and of disapproval are all expressions of a culture.

In relatively balanced periods of history the culture has a sufficiently stable form. The methods and standards which the child has picked up through informal and formal education continue to be reinforced by his later experience, especially where there have been psychological compensations for frustrations that may have been experienced. For instance, girls and women in Victorian society were kept in a relatively subservient position and this by itself would have produced hostility in one form or another, but it had its compensations, at any rate in the higher income groups, where there was a high degree of idealization of women and particularly of the mother. Or to take another and perhaps better example, feudalism, the order of society in which there seemed to be estates fixed by birth, maintained itself for a long time by an implied theocracy. It was like the caste system in that you were called to the estate in which you found yourself and God was on the side of this ordering and so it could not be questioned, for to do so was to question the justice of God himself. Social well-being, therefore, was not a principal consideration because your lot in this world was a preparation for the blessings of heaven if you accepted that the church could guide and aid you in your search for salvation. So the status lines were fixed and for a long time were not seriously questioned. It is no accident that the break-down of the feudal system takes place at a time when Protestantism, the assertion of the individual believer, and capitalism, the individualism of the venturesome financier, also appear in western European history.

Where a society is changing fast, very often what has been learned in early childhood as suitable preparation for adult life does not work. Consider the problem presented by the children of the underground movement during the last war. Their experiences in infancy and early childhood of unsettlement, cunning, fear, initiative and a premature comprehension of events made it virtually impossible for many of them to settle to orderly work after the war. Their childhood experience had been to value survival at all costs, to be prepared for instant improvisation—these are not the norms of a school in peacetime and these children presented their teachers with an acute personal and technical problem.

In a civilization like ours we have to see to it that we prepare children to grow up with a sense of continuity and tradition while at the same time equipping them with a readiness to recognize the need for change and the adaptability and initiative to act. It is interesting to see how the breakaway Protestants of the sixteenth and seventeenth centuries dealt with the changing world which they were in part helping to create. In order to give significance to the individual person in his relationship to God as compared with the institution of the church, which for the Catholic acted as the intermediary, the Protestant shifted the controls which had formerly been outward and visible in the position of the priests to the inward conscience of the believer. This is, of course, a simplification of the matter but it contains a very important transference in the source and power which sanctioned judgment and choice.

The Catholic church has always had a subtle and profound understanding of how to deal with aggression—the priest combines in himself the authority to rebuke and at the same time to offer absolution. The Protestant clergy had no such authority and the individual believer found himself with the privilege and the anxiety of interceding with God direct. The wars of blood, the wars of words between Catholics and Protestants witness to some of the ways in which they dealt with aggression in themselves. With the responsibility for salvation being placed upon the faith or the works of the individual, Protestants took a serious view of pleasure in life and particularly of the necessity to school the wayward desires of the young child. We have here the curious anomaly of individual freedom in religion coupled with guilt and repression. In addition there was the apparent paradox of a distrust of this world's possessions coupled with the belief that worldly success should be accepted as a gift from God.[1]

These comments on the development of Protestantism are admittedly superficial but they indicate how complicated the situation is when we try to plan early education in relation to the need for stability and the need for change. In our society we have to admit that competition and getting ahead are goals apparent throughout the whole range from school examinations to the stock exchange. Conformity, fitting in, being prepared to do what others expect of you, is another and apparently contradictory purpose in our society. But, in fact, these two tendencies represent the poles between which all education has to take shape. On the one hand, originality, creativeness, responsibility, spontaneity—all those qualities which assert the original and the originator in man. On the other, conformity, obedience, subservience, common effort, adjustment—all those qualities which emphasize the willingness to submerge aggressiveness and individuality in the interests of the group and social belongingness.[2]

One of the main points that I have tried to make throughout is that these two tendencies should not be regarded as either/ or activities of man. Too easily we tend to think that when we are exercising one of these qualities it is at the cost of the other. This may be and indeed often is the case but it need not be and in saying this I bring together what the philosopher, the psychologist and the sociologist want of education and we look at our practice and our policy as it takes place in fact and in time.

The philosopher says that we shall work out certain principles in education—such as to develop knowledge, to find methods of testing truth, to offer these opportunities to everyone according to his ability, to recognize that education must also be concerned with growth in feeling as well as in intellect, to provide through curricula and the institutions of society means for appreciating the truth that we are members one of another. Such principles as these represent norms which are here stated in general terms as goals which we should aim at, and as an all-inclusive principle we would say that the educational philosopher has as an aim to provide each person as far as is possible with the conditions in which he may most fully be himself, unique and original.

How are these aims to be realized? We do not spring fully grown into life, we develop biologically and psychologically in ways which can now be broadly understood. There is no quick way to realize any of these aims, they can only be worked out in terms of a child's physiological and psychological endowment and the total environment in which he lives. We now consider that in many cases certain forms of infantile experience make it difficult for the adult to reach the goals which we have already mentioned. There is a psychology of education which can guide us in the handling of younger children and can show us some of the relationships between early experience and its effect in maturity, yet we have to admit that not all our psychological knowledge or the refinement of analysis between cause and effect will enable us to predict and arrange infallibly. There is a dictum which says that education is what a person does with the knowledge that he acquires and while psychology is not expected to take into its orbit any theory of a unique selfhood, those who are engaged in education have special experience of the elusive difference between teaching and learning.

Besides philosophic principles and psychological relationships there is also the unique content of contemporary culture, the environment of the learner. Anyone who wishes to make any pronouncements on how education should be practised has to be prepared to use all the relevant information he can discover from the study of politics, history, economics, the sciences, the arts and so on, because the whole enterprise of education aims at picking out certain essentials from that culture which are thought to be important. What is picked out is in itself partly a result of the effect of the culture upon the teachers; it is also more than merely a personal choice because in each case the institution of the culture as a whole gives us the form and pressure of the times. We can take thought with the best knowledge available as to what the future will be like and part of educational responsibility is to do just this. But we cannot *know*, our forecasts must be more or less informed guesses.

Bearing all this in mind we will seek in education to provide curricula which have sound cultural justifications, a psychological treatment of children which is likely to enable them to judge profitably how to preserve the gap between aspiration and achievement and to be assured enough to want to make judgments about the future. As all these ideas will come from persons, those people will want to know what purposes or goals they should have in mind in making these efforts, and the main purposes I have tried to outline.

Education for spontaneity must lead us on to realize more and more that we are members one of another. If it does not it leads to neurosis and psychosis.

PART FOUR

SOCIOLOGICAL FACTORS

XII

Primary Groups and Their Educational Significance

WE talk about man living in society as though he lived in one omnicompetent group. In fact, of course, he lives in a large number of groups each of which leaves to a greater or less degree its imprint upon his character. For a long time social thought was limited in its outlook because it had only two concepts at its disposal, the individual and society. According to this approach group phenomena were simply individual psychologies multiplied a thousandfold. To substantiate this statement let us look at an example from *The Republic* which might seem at first sight to contradict what we have said.

The allegory of the Cave at the beginning of Book VII has been mentioned earlier and it would appear that one of the purposes of this parable is to divide men into appropriate groups. But really Plato's concern is to describe the progress of the mind towards the discovery of the Form of the Good. There are some who live in the depths of a cave, chained and facing towards its inner wall; there is behind them a raised roadway and beyond that a wall. Men pass on the roadway carrying objects and beyond the roadway and wall there is a huge fire, so that the shadows of the objects which the men carry are thrown on to the inner wall to be seen by the inhabitants. Similarly the voices and words of the men on the road echo back from the inner wall. This, says Plato, is the common lot of all of us early in our lives and for many of us through our whole life. Most men live all their lives underground seeing nothing but shadows, hearing nothing but echoes. The philosopher alone has made his way out of this cave into the light of the sun above ground and he is the only person who can compare with reality the shadows over which the men in the cave quarrel, he is the only one who can compare the light of the fire with the light of the sun. The things which we quarrel over in our daily life in law courts and parliaments are the shadows of reality.

The Form of the Good is a source of existence to all objects of knowledge and it is this Form which enables man's mind to know these objects and which at the same time is in itself the highest object of knowledge. Plato's concern is to find the choice spirits who can undertake the rigours of discovery. Glaucon and Socrates are conducting the conversation in which all these things are discussed. At one point Socrates says:

'It will be our task . . . to compel the best natures to proceed to that study which we declared a little while ago to be the highest, to perceive the good and to make that ascent we spoke of; and when they have done so and looked long enough then we must not allow them the liberty which they now enjoy . . . the liberty of staying there and refusing to descend again to the prisoners and to share with them in toils and honours whether they be mean or exalted.'

He goes on to say of these guardians that they have been begotten for the city as well as for themselves. To be like leaders and kings in a hive, they have received a better and more thorough education than other philosophers and are more capable of participating both in public life and in philosophy.[1]

In this allegory we have a description of how the ruling group is to be discovered and later in the book we find how they are to be educated for their responsibilities. Plato is not concerned about the effect which belonging to this group will have upon its members. He describes in great detail the qualities which they will need to have and the training which they must undergo but he is writing a treatise in moral philosophy not a study in psychology or sociology.

Novelists in the seventeenth, eighteenth and nineteenth centuries have come nearer to understanding group phenomena, and writers like Defoe and Jane Austen have an acute sense of behaviour and response to convention. It is only in the nineteenth century when we begin to see the rise of sociological thought that we become aware that group phenomena are not simply individual psychologies multiplied a thousandfold but that there is an immense variety of group formations and each of them has a different impact upon the individual's behaviour.

Comte, Marx and Spencer may be considered as among those who began to think systematically about society and the workings of groups within society. In addition the contributions of social geographers, of humanitarians, of novelists within the last century or so have enabled us to regard as a commonplace that the child behaves differently in the family, with his play fellows and in the classroom and that in many particulars the adult behaves differently in his office, at home and at his club. It is always ihe changing nature of these group organizations which elicits appropriate ways of behaviour.

C. H. Cooley made the distinction between primary and secondary groups and according to his analysis the prototype of a primary group is the family.[2] This is the group in which our most intimate, spontaneous and varied life is lived. It is the nursery of human nature in which what Cooley and other American sociologists have called, face-to-face personal relationships prevail. Obviously the play group, the neighbourhood, the classroom, the church and the village offer some of the qualities of life to be found in the primary group.

Secondary groups are those in which members come only into indirect contact with each other through formal relationships (as in the case of delegates at a conference) or through reports or hearsay or by some other secondhand contact. The characteristic of secondary grouping is that it is difficult for the persons concerned to make any real contact with one another and they have to be satisfied with a functional and fragmentary relationship. Large-scale organizations whether industrial or educational or political are bound to offer relationships mainly of this secondary group type.

It is in the family, the play group, the primary group that we first acquire our personality traits. We pick them up through the face-to-face contacts which are our daily experience and in our early childhood we imitate the specific behaviour that we see in loved ones and we do not for a number of years find ourselves guided by abstract ideals. For instance we do not

begin to tell the truth or behave decently because we understand what our parents mean when they tell us in so many
words to be truthful or to behave nicely, we do it because they
have shown us the ways of behaving which are considered to be
truthful or nice and we try to imitate these. As a result of our
membership of this primary group we have many experiences
of specific actions and attitudes and our later ideals are usually
connected with this primary imagery. We have already
sufficiently considered the dependence of adult models on
childhood experience not to need to elaborate it further here.

Besides the individual and precise experience which membership of primary groups offers to us in the early formation of our
personality, it also presents us with our first experience of social
unity and social behaviour. How far shall we stick to our own
property and refuse to share what we have; shall we play with
other children and learn to co-operate with them in other ways,
or shall we fight them? The primary attitudes of sympathy,
love, resentment, ambition, vanity, hero worship, sense of social
justice, or right and wrong in general, kindness, equity, honesty,
deference to public opinion, fear of ridicule—these and many
other primary attitudes have their roots in our early experience
and they are found in varying forms in every society, not because they are innate instincts necessarily but because all
societies have primary groups, especially that of the family and
in such groups qualities like those I have mentioned above
develop spontaneously because without them people could not
live together in any degree of amity or happiness. It is no accident that nearly all religious codes contain primary virtues.

With the development of wider contact groups our experience
is extended well beyond the family and specific experiences
and we begin to build up more generalized responses in the form
of moral principles and abstract ideals. So the generalizations
which seem to govern the life of larger social organizations
develop very gradually from primary attitudes and images as
these become expanded and more elaborate. Take as an instance
the teachings of Christianity, many of which are the primary
attitudes of the family projected into a wider society. The ideas
of love, mutual help, loyalty, kindness and meekness are those
which appear in family life at its best. Christ taught that he
wished these virtues to become the basis of our public institu-

tions and of society in the large. Taken literally, to love everybody as a brother is impossible but if we extract the principle which underlies this ideal, it might become the basis of our social institutions. Reinhold Niebuhr in his book *An Interpretation of Christian Ethics* called this kind of precept 'an impossible possibility'. It is certainly true that our social services care for people in need and democratic principles have their origin in the vision of equity, equality and justice. These virtues are present in man, not because they are innate instincts but because mutual help, justice and loyalty form the basis of family life and we have never rid ourselves of the appeal and power of these demands even when in later life we have found them continually violated. It is a truism of western civilization to say that most of all we desire peace and friendship—nobody prefers war and destructiveness even though they may feel still that they are bound to engage in them. The warrior is no longer a desirable model for the infant growing up in a democratic society.

In a simple community of a few families the ideals of democracy may be practised in their primary form. As the society grows, the contacts widen, the intimate groups give place to a certain amount of abstract organization and to living at a psychological distance from one another. Nevertheless the primary ideals which have been experienced in the simple community are likely to be translated into abstract terms. For instance, the principle of economic justice appears in the ideal of a state whose duty it is to protect the weak and to promote equality of opportunity through universal education and to be responsible for the control of industry and finance. The improvement of society as we know it does not really call for any essential change in the values in human nature or any radical re-making of man, it calls chiefly for a wider and wider application of man's family impulses and this at least we can learn from Cooley's analysis. To realize in this way the significance of primary groups prepares ground for a better understanding of the family and its influence, and the sociologist today is not satisfied simply to point to some general functions of the family in society at large.

The comments made so far would tend to indicate that primary qualities are all good ones and this, of course, need not be the case. When children go into school they take with them the values and attitudes from their homes and teachers have to be prepared to detect the positive and negative influences in the background of their pupils. As an example of what I mean let us examine the report produced by the White House Conference on Child Health and Protection which in 1936 considered the topic *The Young Child in the Home*.[3] This was a survey of about 3,000 families selected as a national sample. They were rated as to socio-economic status and the background and interests of the children were found to correlate closely with economic level. Seven classes were distinguished and for purposes of sharp comparison we shall outline some of the findings related to Class 1, the professional group and to Class 7, the urban and rural day labourers.

First of all, permanency of residence decreases as we move down the scale from Class 1 to Class 7. One-half of the families in the first class own their own homes, only one-fourth in the seventh class. Almost all the first class homes have over five rooms and less than a fifth of Class 7 families are so placed. Play apparatus was found in three-quarters of the gardens of the first class homes but only in one-third of the homes in Class 7. The lower in the socio-economic scale the investigators went the poorer became the parents' health and the poorer the health of the children. Over half of the upper class mothers consulted doctors about their children as compared with one-tenth at the lower level—this is not surprising in the American context where medical care is very expensive and where specialization amongst doctors is much more common than in England.

All the infants in the first class were fed regularly as compared with two-thirds in Class 7 and it is interesting to note that less milk was drunk by children of the farmer group (they were actually placed in Class 4) than by children in either the first or seventh class. The youngsters in the first class went to bed earlier and slept longer than those at the lower levels. In fact, the children in Class 7 showed a superiority in only one point—they dressed themselves at an earlier age.

All the children who were studied seemed to have much the same kind of fears but the methods of removing them differed. In Class 1, two-thirds of the children had the situations explained to them and it was expected that the parents would help the children to understand what was happening and so their fears would disappear. In Class 7 this occurred with only two-fifths of the children. As to the methods of child control, reasoning and punishment by depriving the child of some pleasures were very commonly found in the first class and these two methods decreased in frequency as we move down the scale, and they are replaced by scolding and whipping.

Fragmentary as this summary is, nevertheless, it shows the very wide variations in the conditions to be found in the home and in the cultural worlds opened up to children. Opportunities for child development favour the upper class from the moment of their birth and it is substantially true to say that a child has little chance to develop a wider background of interests than his parents permit him to. If his parents are incompetent or unfortunate, so much the worse for the child.

The White House Conference Study also considered the influence of what it called 'accord' homes and 'discord' homes and their general conclusion was that as a rule the 'accord' home provides the child with protection, security, guidance and encouragement. It gives practice with the methods of group living and it gives a good grounding in conventional moral standards. It makes some attempt to interpret the outside world to the child, to explain what is happening and to temper the wind to the shorn lamb.

'Discord' homes have much the opposite effects. They are marked by persistent conflict and divergence of aims between the parents, the child seldom gains a sense of family unity and hence its personal security is much more precarious. If he obeys one parent or patterns himself on that parent's conduct the child finds himself at cross purposes with the other parent and if he compares his home with other homes and his treatment with the treatment given to other children he comes to be acutely dissatisfied with what he has and to regard his parents as unfit for their task. So with this feeling of inadequacy in his background, unable very often to advance his own plans and ambitions, he may find himself a rebel within his home and perhaps a delinquent outside, or at any rate, a person who feels that he has had an unjust deal from his family and from society as a whole.

Goodwin Watson in a comparison of the effects of lax and strict training in the home has some interesting things to say about the home which demands too much of the children.[4] Watson had as his sample 260 graduate students and of these 60 per cent. were judged to come from strict homes, which were defined in terms of a number of items like severe punishment, regular insistence on bedtime, compulsory Sunday School attendance and the like. Even in terms of the early 'thirties it is perhaps interesting that three-fifths of the graduate students (that is to say not undergraduates in British terms, but those who have completed a first degree), came from such homes. For us to get the full value from these and other types of investigation we should want to know more about the university background, because, of course, in the United States a number of universities are denominational foundations and still maintain a certain strictness in behaviour. But for the time being that is not the important issue in this matter of the influence of strict and lax homes on later behaviour and attitudes. The students who came from repressive homes showed a much greater dislike of their parents than those who came from either a lax or the average home group. As might be expected they showed a greater degree of infantile dependence earlier on in their lives and even into their early adulthood and they were more quarrelsome than average in their social relationships and had more fear, guilt and anxiety to contend with. In their childhood they seemed to have fewer playmates and more make-believe play companions than other children and the same kind of social pattern shows later because they have fewer friends in adolescence and, within terms of the American culture, they seemed to experience more broken engagements. Much of their behaviour was characterized by uncertainty and indecision and this appeared in unsettled attitudes toward their vocation, both before they had come to a decision about it and after they had begun on the job of their choice. In short, the strict demands which were made on them in their infancy and childhood, by which their parents presumably expected to establish a firm personality structure, had led to later unsettlement, anxiety and self-doubt greater than the average.

L. A. Cook, in his book *Community Backgrounds in Education*, has a great deal of valuable information on the relationship between early family experience of the child and his later personality development. In common with most other social researchers he reports that going to school may be regarded from the point of view of the young child as a major crisis because he passes from a range of familiar contact into a new and strange world in which he has no guarantee that he will be regarded with affection or be given the security which in a good home he has already received. If on the other hand, his infancy has been disturbed and troubled at home he carries the expectation of anxiety and conflict with him into the novel scheme of life which he finds in school.[5] It is characteristic of all schools that by reason of numbers and the purpose for which the institution is in existence at all they must be more impersonal than a family, more routinized and in many cases more authoritarian. It is interesting to note that in England nursery and infant schools have on the whole accepted a permissive and more or less informal way of life, though even here the routine has of necessity to be established from the beginning. Nevertheless, the subject matter is presented in as varied and stimulating a way as possible and the children are taught in small groups with teaching aids aimed to enliven the material with which they have to deal.

In the junior school, between the ages of seven and eleven, the transition is made from this more informal approach to knowledge to the organized content of the secondary school. It follows, therefore, that a junior school having a double aim is in a particularly critical position in relation to the educational growth of any child because it looks back at the more spontaneous child-centred practice of the infant school and forward to the well-defined curricula of the secondary school. It would be very easy for the junior school to be broken-backed in its aims and if, as Dewey and others have insisted, it is important to treat the child as a being and not a becoming, this can be a special problem for teachers in junior schools.

The young child beginning school has to accustom himself to the authority of the teacher, an adult who has a responsibility to be just and fair to 30 or 40 youngsters and who therefore must be more dominant and less personally affectionate than parents to individual children. However, there is a truth in the opposite direction, too, in that one teacher disseminating her influence over 30 to 40 children may prove to be more reassuring and less frightening than a domineering parent who can make her influence felt more intensively in a family of two or three.

One of the principal tasks of the school right from the start is to enable the child to come to terms with authority and the image of the schoolmaster frequently created in literature suggests that he is too often dominating and cruel. As we shall see when we go on to consider the situation inside the school, there has to be by definition a dominance-submission relationship between the teacher and his pupil. The form which this relationship takes can of course vary very widely and it is important to stress that while these terms dominance and submission are used they are intended to be purely descriptive and not to carry with them the emotional overtones which would make dominance mean domineering and submission mean submissive. We have in mind simply that the teacher is an adult who has been given the responsibility of instructing children who are put in his charge for the purpose of learning and it is for the children to appreciate sooner rather than later what the nature of the relationship is. Coming as they do from the family situation where in any case the adults have greater responsibility than the children and authority over them, it is quite reasonable to expect that the children as pupils will accept the position of authority which their teachers hold.

I do not want at this point to anticipate a fuller discussion of this whole matter which comes later, but it is important that we should understand that a child going to school for the first time will carry with him, and needs to carry with him, the experiences of parental authority which will be the chart by which he gauges what this new adult, the teacher, will expect of him.

Infant schools recognize the enormous importance of the reception class in helping children to establish themselves in this new setting because, after all, besides the relationship to the adults, there is the large-scale adaptation to many other children of their own age. Most children have had plenty of experience of playing with two or three of their contemporaries but have never found themselves together with thirty or forty, let alone several hundreds, which is the situation in the classroom and in the school as a whole and it is not infrequent to find that some newcomers to the infant school take a good time to build up the confidence which will enable them to play with any degree of assurance with groups of other children. Withdrawal behaviour is reasonably often met with in which the child either physically tries to avoid all others and stay by himself or even if he is with others, seems to live, as we say, in a world of his own into which he has obviously decided that if he cannot withdraw physically, he is quite free to withdraw psychologically.

In everyday terms we often say that children must grow up and we very often forget the painful experiences which this meant for ourselves at various stages in our life. Going to school is certainly one of these because at this time the child may be suffering from feelings of insecurity and inferiority and longing for the assurance and shelter of the home. We have said all along that the attitudes which children build up in the first five years of life are important to them in adolescence and in adulthood. It is equally true to say that the experiences that children have in the early days of their school life are of the greatest significance for their consequent feelings for school and what goes on there.[6]

While it is true that at all times there should be a close contact between the school and the home so that some kind of common strategy may be agreed upon, this is never more true than in the early years and Cook differentiates three types of home which he calls co-operative-to-school homes, antagonistic-to-school homes and average homes between these extremes. The co-operative-to-school home seeks to ally itself with the purposes of the school, to send the child on time, dressed as required, and with the necessary equipment. It takes an interest in what goes on in the school and wants to find out how the child is getting on and the parents make a point of becoming acquainted with the children's teachers. Such a home regards the reports of the school with good sense as helpful comments on the child's development and seeks to fit in with health requirements and to recognize that the picture which the teachers may have of the child's potentialities, if it differs from the parent's picture, is likely to be based on actual performance and therefore merits close consideration. In short, it regards the school as engaged with the home in a co-operative effort in the upbringing of children and credits the teachers with good intentions and good sense. If such parents find the treatment of the school deserves criticism they have the assurance to expect that their point of view will be fairly considered.

Antagonistic-to-school homes are pretty well the opposite of those just mentioned. By precept and example they side with the child in seeming to encourage a slipshod attitude to the school's requirements—for instance, attendance may be poor, punctuality lax and there may be hostility on the part of the parents to the teachers. In fact there is little if any sense of common purpose between the adults in the case.

Obviously these two kinds of homes are extremes and in between there is a wide range of attitudes ranging from tolerant interest to relative indifference. Very often the indifferent parents have come to regard the teachers as the experts who are mainly responsible for the intellectual and social development of children. For instance, blame for social breakdown is often attached to the school and we are all aware of the kind of criticism which compares the amount of money spent on education with the relative increase in juvenile delinquency. I have tried to emphasize throughout this book that the school is only one of the institutions concerned with education and that it has to deal with a personality structure in its pupils which has already been substantially formed.

The antagonistic-to-school home really has no idea of education at all. It lives from hand to mouth in a perpetual attitude of getting by in life and for it the school has nothing to offer and it is difficult to see what other institution has anything to give either. In the average home, however, there seems to be a fragmented and incomplete view of what education is because in handing over so much to the school and by ignoring their complementary responsibilities such homes assume that education is a matter of instruction which can be carried out by trained people who prescribe the exercises and see that they are carried through. The notion of the personality of the learner and the quality of his initiative and how it is affected by the rest of his life experiences does not enter into this interpretation of education and neither does the idea of education as a part of a whole culture.

It is well to recognize that some of the functions of school make it difficult for the parents to maintain a disinterested and friendly attitude to the school and its teachers. For instance, at the secondary stage, and in England at the junior stage before selection for secondary education takes place, the function of the school as a selective agency is very clear. If a child is to qualify to go to a university in order to enter upon a future professional career, it is necessary for him to pass required examinations and to do this in England it is necessary to be placed in a secondary grammar school—or at least it is very usual. Naturally as the adolescent moves towards the end of his school life and the question of his future career has to be seriously considered, the examination record of the school is often uppermost, and co-operative-to-school homes through the interest and maybe the anxiety of the parents tend to bring a concealed pressure to bear on the purposes of the school. As an example, it is sometimes difficult for the head of a grammar school to try to maintain an interest in the general education of his sixth-form pupils when the parents want to make the adolescents concentrate on their examination subjects, and not only the parents but the universities or institutions of higher education in general by reason of the demands which they make for entry.

Schools with a history in which generations of fathers and sons or mothers and daughters may have been educated, are often in a more powerful position to influence, at any rate the parents, than is the case with newer schools or with families who may not previously have had any connection with a grammar school and who are now anxious that the first generation in the grammar school should 'get on'.

We need not emphasize the obvious importance in obtaining a sense of common purpose between the home and the school. The numerous occasions on which parents are invited to come to the school to see displays of the work done, to witness the plays produced or to hear the music, are all helpful in enabling the parents to see for themselves and to understand what the school is after. Similarly parent-teachers' associations are means of ensuring that parents may find out what is going on in the school and how their children are performing, but likewise such associations offer opportunities for the parents to come together as an interested body of adults who may in their turn offer help of many different kinds to the school. In such ways the school can be seen not simply as a place where qualifications may be gained for the future but as a community of children who have families behind them who are linked together in this educational society. In other words, the school can become much more of a primary group.

In our school system the nursery and infant schools work together with the home more than at any other stage and there is frequently a strong interest in a child's career particularly towards the end of the secondary stage. The relationships between home and school in this country are at their weakest while the child is between the ages of eight and fourteen, that is to say in the second half of his junior school experience and the first part of his secondary school years.

If the family is interested in education this will show itself in many different ways, not only in the concern which parents may feel for their children at the school and their desire to co-operate. It may appear in the activities of the parents on governing bodies or in local affairs related to education. Adult education as an organized system in Britain has a long and honourable history but it is true to say that its influence has been exerted on a relatively small number of people. The new mass media have brought an entirely different situation into being both for children and adults. Only adults may attend lectures given in formal courses for them but the material in television and on the radio is available in most homes. It is true that there is a censorship of sorts on the cinema but if children wish to buy any publication, provided they have the money, they can usually do so. The cultural idiosyncrasies of different age groups are now brought much more closely together than before. It is possible for us now to see and hear through television and radio and the cinema what other adults think children enjoy and it is possible for young people to discover what they think of adults' interests. This may lead to greater understanding or greater hostility because it used to be the case that while adults recognized that adolescents had interests which were up to a point their own affair, provided they conducted them out of sight and perhaps even more out of earshot of the adults, it is not now possible for adults to cut these expressions off so neatly, hence the problem of greater understanding or greater hostility.

Parents in these days have the opportunity to learn more about the care and upbringing of children than has ever been the case before. Women's magazines for all levels of ability and background, the radio, television, child welfare clinics, ante-natal and post-natal care of children—through these means and many others information of an informed kind is passed on. In girls' schools we now have a comprehensive course in domes-tic studies and even in grammar schools where there has been a tendency to prepare the intellectually abler girls in academic studies only, teachers now recognize much more than they used to that they have a responsibility to the future girl under-graduate as a wife and mother as well.

The potential for the mutual recognition by the home and the school of their interdependence is greater than it has ever been. Similarly it is now possible to discern the meaning of education writ large through society as a whole. Not long ago educators were pointing out the need for the cultivation of individual interests because in the future with automation and the reduced number of working hours, more leisure time would be available to most of us and unless we had strongly developed individual interests it was thought that increased leisure might turn out to be a doubtful blessing. This is of course still true and more clearly obvious than ever. As we have tended to plan and organize our society more and more and to channel off many of the activities which were previously left in the hands of individuals to institutions like schools, universities, technical colleges, colleges of further education and the like, we have come to see that the principle of compulsory general education will need to be further scrutinized. We now take it so much for granted in Great Britain that a child should go to school at five and leave at fifteen (soon to be sixteen) and that full-time education is necessary for a good deal longer in the case of those people who are going into the professions or entering an apprenticeship that we scarcely notice that this compulsory requirement has been in existence for only just over half a century, if we take 1880 as the first point at which any real attempt to ensure compulsory attendance began.

In the future we may have to reorganize our thinking about

131

'attending school' quite radically. After all, before 1870 or 1880 it was thought to be quite normal for children to start working at four or five years of age, at any rate in certain classes in our society and it took some time for the idea of compulsory education for everybody to gain acceptance. Economic and social events as much as humanitarian principle made it necessary for our ancestors to initiate compulsory schooling. The number of years of this type of schooling has been consequent upon the needs of the society and the amount of preparation necessary to prepare for useful occupations. It has also been dependent upon the amount of money which the society has been prepared to commit to the erection of buildings and the payment either directly or indirectly of teachers, the provision of equipment and the like. At present we require our pupils to have ten years of compulsory education and in the case of about 20 per cent. of them we expect eleven or thirteen years at school and in many cases an additional three or four years at a place of higher education. By the time a doctor is qualified he has completed eighteen or nineteen of his twenty-three or twenty-four years *in statu pupillari*.

In relation to the country's needs in food, manufactured articles and services of all kinds the years of preparation, whether full-time or part-time are purely relative. Education is not instruction but has far wider and deeper intentions—we have considered this whole matter in the first section of this book, and it is quite obvious that the more man makes machines do his work for him, the less time he will need to spend working for his livelihood. This brings enormous problems to mind which we cannot consider in any detail here. The main point which I wish to make is that we have not really begun to consider what we can do in adult education for the nation at large. The English tradition in education has developed out of the education of the minority, of 'the quality', and it is only now beginning to realize the problems which education for equality, for the masses, raises.

There are two points of view on this matter. First the point of view of the ordinary man who thinks of education primarily as a means of preparation for a career and who associates it with the prelude to the serious business of earning one's living. This is the direct consequence of the precept of schooling as a hard-won privilege of the lower orders who might otherwise expect to spend their waking life from an early age in gainful employment. The second point of view is that of the professional educator who sees his responsibility as only in part to prepare his pupils for their future employment and who in many cases regards his more ultimate and more rewarding purpose as helping them to develop their own potentialities as students and as persons. The pressure of a competitive society and indeed of a world where half the population is still living at or below the subsistence level, makes it very difficult for this second point of view to prevail in any widespread way. Yet the trend in western society is to reduce the actual time spent by each person in earning his living and by inventions in the mass media to provide more and more opportunities for passing the time.

The crux of the whole matter is whether we can manage to convince ourselves and future generations that there is a difference between education and passing the time and that we must use all possible agencies to enrich education not only during a period of what we become used to as compulsory education but through the voluntary acceptance of the compulsive quality of education during the whole of life.

As this point of view begins to establish itself, so the whole question of the relationship between the family and education is transformed because no longer is the main and significant period of education concentrated into the period of compulsory schooling so that parents have to take a deliberate interest in the school when in most cases they have themselves long ceased to have personal contact with education in any formal way. Looking at education in this new way means that it is indeed a part of life in which each member of the family, whatever his age, expects to be active.

XIII

Sociology and the Classroom*

In Western Europe schools have locations, buildings, some
definiteness and permanence and from this material point
of view they are local features, landmarks known for themselves and known as examples of similar buildings in the county
and the country, indeed as a sign of such buildings throughout
other lands too. Yet while we take for granted that schools must
have location, buildings and equipment, in Australia, New
Zealand, Canada and elsewhere there are 'radio schools'
where the children work in their own homes, forming groups
separated by perhaps hundreds of miles, who yet are in a sense
a school class following a common programme. In countries
where the terrain is difficult and the distances vast, boarding
schools are obviously one answer. But the resources of the
'radio school' and the possibilities of the 'television school',
force us to reconsider what a school is.

The schools contain a selected population. In this country,
leaving aside nursery schools, the main people to be found in
schools are children and adolescents from five to eighteen.
There is a much smaller proportion of adults and these have
positions of greater or less authority in relation to the children
—compare for example the position of the head of a school and
its caretaker. All normal children between the ages of five and
fifteen have to have full-time education of some sort. A compulsion is placed upon them by law and full-time education
means an occupation for the larger part of the day throughout
most of the year—as it has sometimes been expressed, going
to school is to work for your living without being paid for it.

* This chapter is more freely improvised from Professor Mannheim's notes
than any of the others.—W.A.C.S.

The school has three main functions. The first is to present certain data which are regarded as being important. By whom is the selection of these data made? By the officers of the local education authority, by the teachers' panels, by individual teachers, by headmasters, by Her Majesty's Inspectors, by professional bodies, by educational thinkers and writers, sometimes by school managers and governors and often by public opinion in one form or another. Obviously not all these forces are equally important nor are they all experienced at the same time, but while it is true to say that in Great Britain the teacher has an unusual degree of freedom as compared with educational practice in some other countries, it is a fallacy to suggest that teachers are free to teach what they like. They themselves are the products of a culture and there is what we might call an educational sub-culture of constraining and approved theory and practice.

After the presentation of these data, which are regarded as important, the second main function of the school is to encourage certain attitudes thought to be helpful in getting on with the business of learning and also valuable to the child in his present and future life as a person. The third main function is, of course, to help to prepare the pupil in a number of ways for his later career.

The school has also a number of indirect functions, the first of which is to use the dependent years of childhood and adolescence to 'train' and prepare for adult life. Following from this the subordination of children prolongs their economic dependency and so tends to keep them 'young'. Authority is given to the adults and so changes are made reasonably gradually. It was interesting to see how in war-time this prevailing pattern had to change. Warfare is a young man's business and many positions of authority cannot be put into the hands of men who expect to hold them until they retire at sixty-five. The armed forces have a completely different position in the prestige system of the country in time of war and high abilities of all kinds are drawn together so that the thirty-year-old colonels, group captains and naval commanders find themselves in positions of unprecedented authority and esteem. In a democratic country like Great Britain which has not a strong tradition of an officer class, to provide authority to men of ability when most of them could not expect to attain that distinction in their peace-time occupations, creates seismic changes in the distribution of power. During war-time these are concealed in the larger loyalty but they re-emerge in a thousand different ways in peace-time.

The third indirect function of school is that it encourages people to believe that education should be equated with the institutions which provide formal instruction of one kind or another. There is then a tendency to think that education is always something provided by experts, or at least people with an appropriate training—this is in fact the narrow concept of education which was contrasted earlier in this book with the broader view of an educative society and while it is true that schooling represents one other pattern of formative juvenile experience as general as experience in the family, the purposes of school are far more defined and limited than the spontaneous relationships of a family can possibly be. We can make this point very clearly if we look more closely at a school actually at work.

Let us first of all look at a class of thirty-five twelve-year-old children. How are they organized? Throughout their school careers they will be grouped with their contemporaries and so they will become accustomed to having the limitations and oddities of each age group intensified. They sit in desks usually, often in rows, all facing one way, although contemporary furniture and classroom organization is tending to change this. This basic grid of rows and aisles helps to define the area of attention somewhat and enables the teacher placed at the front of the class and usually with a somewhat higher desk, possibly a dais, to supervise the class and when necessary to become a focus of attention. The desk helps to indicate the sobriety of behaviour expected, the rows to show the neatness of planning and habits which teachers hope to see appearing in their pupils and the formation represents as a whole a 'unit' for class teaching and many teachers would feel uneasy if they had not these rows to deal with—they might consider that the classroom would then become slovenly and unbusiness-like, at least in appearance.

If we turn to the teacher we find that he is an adult who is in the Euclidean sense 'given'. He did not choose to teach this group of pupils and they did not select him as their tutor. At the beginning of the acquaintanceship the pupils and the teacher are strangers to one another who have come together for business reasons. While the pupils are normally expected to stay at their desks and get on with their work as required, the teacher has freedom to move around as need suggests, to help, to reprove or to supervise.

These physical relationships are important because they give the very often unexamined basic framework on which classroom relationships and the teacher-pupil-work attitudes are built up. There is of course also what one might call a mental organization within the classroom. The children are graded according to ability so that learning may be easier and selection is part of the school's function and has sound psychological grounds, but the psychological motives are often not understood or are overlooked by many parents, employers, and even teachers. For them selection and grading exist in order to promote competition which has as its main aim to sort out the best from the intellectual point of view. Grading is not regarded as an aid to more efficient teaching but rather as a means of indicating degrees of 'success' and 'failure'. If we might put this in another way, grading from the psychological point of view is regarded as good because it provides a group which is comparable in range whatever its level and therefore teaching can be arranged more economically and effectively. Sociologically, grading for many people in our competitive society means simply to try to discover the best. For the psychologist or for the psychologically minded teacher, grading is a means of discovering who should be able to work together and thus competition is being used as a device which will enable the teacher to encourage co-operation later at whatever intellectual level. Where selection is used as a means of assessing competence for various purposes (as it quite legitimately may be) it is an instrument for exclusion which is necessary when there are more applicants than there are vacancies. This is, of course, the crux of the whole issue of selection for secondary education in England. The psychologist regards this as a grading operation, the socially minded parent in our competitive society often regards it as an assessment of success or failure and the question of co-operation at a later date does not enter into the matter.

In a sense the timetable is also a physical organization but we shall consider it here from the point of view of mental organization as well. Attendance at school is compulsory and the day is organized and when people talk of freedom in education they must first of all admit that as with all human freedom it is limited. The very concept of school and its function is a limit on the freedom of individual spontaneity and once we admit that we can begin to discuss realistically how to enable education to be as free and flexible as possible. Pupils arrive at a certain time, they leave at a certain time. They have so long for recess, or break, or significantly 'playtime', and so long as a break for dinner, or equally significantly, lunch. The day is split up into periods and as the pupils change from one to the other they must (or rather they are expected to) turn their attention to whatever 'they' elect to teach. There may be six or eight or more of these changes a day and the pupils are frequently exhorted to pay attention and not to waste time. In other words they are expected to learn what they may not wish to learn because they have seldom any say in its choice.

The pupils are collected in a classroom group so' that they may be taught certain data (this is not to say that they learn them). They are checked and corrected in various ways to see that they have in fact done the work and this we may call after Freud the manifest content of the classroom. Behind this obvious appearance there is the routine of attendance, punctuality, self-submergence to authority, the silence of the class, the recognition of hierarchy—prefects, teachers, head teachers. These factors represent the latent. content, the underlying effect of the organization of school. What I have called the manifest content of school work is represented by active learning. The latent content is represented by passive learning, the habits, data, attitudes picked up through constant, familiar, steady contact with a state of affairs we do not have to think about.

There is a common interaction between the thirty-five twelve-year-olds at their desks and the one teacher facing them. The teacher is an adult, above average in intelligence, trained for a number of years to know his subject matter and how to teach it. For the practical purposes of the children he selects what to teach and he works to a timetable. As an adult he is separated from the range of his pupils by physique, experience, responsibility, competence, status, dress, manners, manner and appearance. The teacher is not the 'natural' leader of his group —only children in the group, spontaneously chosen either by election or by acceptance of their superiority, can be that, since they start with relatively similar endowments and problems as their fellows and are drawn into their positions by the faith that the led have in their leader's competence. Not so however with the teacher. The classroom is a pattern of relationships in which a leader is needed, whose official responsibility is already decided. Personal leadership or natural leadership arises when somebody leads spontaneously, being readier to act, more unexpected and complex, maybe more ruthless, than the led and he can very often break conventions at need. The institutional leader may not do this because he has an expected pattern of behaviour to follow and the conventional framework in which to operate—as one writer has it, his personal influence must be strained through the sieve of formality.

The teacher is an institutional leader in the first place. Prestige attaches to the office and not, at any rate initially, to the person. He is supposed to be the acknowledged superior in the pupil-teacher relationship and authority rests not so much in him as a person as in the laws and traditions of his office. Obviously with a successful teacher the element of personal leadership will grow greater and greater as time passes but this kind of acceptance he has to seek after and to deserve, for it entails a presentation of a personality enlarged beyond the classroom and not wholly to be contained within it. For instance, the martinet makes himself a classroom and school figure who does not properly relate to the pupils' world outside.

When our thirty-five twelve-year-olds meet their new teacher, the first requirement implicit in the relationship is of dominance-submission and we have seen how the physical placing aims at this. Waller in his valuable book *The Sociology of Teaching* puts the requirement as drastically as this.

'Until the teacher's definition of the situation has been accepted he cannot relax. Friendly attitudes must spring up only in a situation defined in terms of teacher domination.'*[1]

* Mannheim valued this book highly and his notes contain many extracts from it. I have drawn on parts of it in sections of this chapter. W.A.C.S.

So bald a statement may perturb many people and it is the antithesis of the principles of Homer Lane[2] and A. S. Neill[3] and those implied in the title of a book such as *The Child is Right*.[4] Nevertheless, Waller's view only states what happens in most schools and let it be noticed how wide the variation may be within the terms of the statement. What he is saying is simply that, since the teacher has the knowledge, the responsibility for planning how to communicate that knowledge and a group of children who may not wish to learn what he presents, some kind of final authority and incentive has to be submerged in the group. This authority, says Waller, is vested in the teacher and his power is potentially great because he has in the last resort the authority of the law and the government to back his position. In another place Waller says:

'The political organization of the school is one which makes the teacher dominant and it is his business to use that dominance to further the process of teaching and learning.'[5]

This dominance-submission aspect is a basic condition of the relationship between the teacher and his pupils. Even if it is arrived at by Neill's methods of waiting for inner development in the child, the final recognition that this adult has something to give for which his pupils must accept conditions which will allow him to teach them, has to be made.

The school is in business to teach and to enable pupils to learn and Ross Finney puts it like this,

'The [primary] purpose of school is to pass on cognitive capital. Only secondarily is it for getting young people together.'[6]

Of course because they *are* together the young people and their elders do in fact strike up human relationships of all kinds and here we move into the field of psychology. The difference between psychological and sociological relationships is that in the first you are concerned with the content of, the changes and motives in, human experience. In sociology you are concerned more with the structure of the groupings in which the content, changes and motives express themselves. There is of course a borderland of social psychology which is in both territories where the difference is really one of emphasis rather than of point of view, and this territory of human relationships between teacher and pupils is in this borderland because from one point of view we are concerned with the content of human attitude and experience and from another we are interested in the kind of grouping and organization which gives direction to these psychological processes.

The teacher brings into the classroom his views of his job, his prejudices, his personal fears and inadequacies, his ambitions, his humanity and affection. The thirty-five twelve-year-olds whom he has to teach differ in physique, appearance, intelligence, sociability, temperament and social and personal background. They have the chance unity of a class and after a time together they begin to develop a sense of solidarity and a working compromise with the teacher, an important person in this total group. The age of the children, their standing *vis-à-vis* the other pupils in the school and the degree of responsibility given to them by their teachers, make a great deal of difference to the influence they have upon the school and the school has upon them. For instance, twelve-year-old boys in a preparatory school where the oldest boy is thirteen or fourteen are in a very different case from their contemporaries at the bottom of a grammar school whose oldest boy is eighteen.

How does the human interaction between our thirty-five twelve-year-olds and their teacher grow? In most cases as the teacher in the end wishes. He has the major instruments of control in his hands and if he is unable to make them work, then a situation of chronic conflict grows up in which authority and control have been broken down. When we say that the human interaction grows in most cases as the teacher wishes we do not want to suggest that he is in command of all that happens, which would be both drastically wrong and impossible in any case. But it is he who is in a position to decide more than anyone else what sort of classroom this is going to be and while it is true that in school, as elsewhere, teachers are what the other people in the group expect them and allow them to be, nevertheless, the social structure of the school weights the dice heavily in favour of the teacher. Some wise words by Waller bear repetition here: 'In the most happily conducted institutions all the teachers and some of the leading students feel that they have a very real voice in the conduct of school affairs.'[7]

A properly worked out sociological view of the classroom has always to bear in mind the often submerged, out-of-school life of the children, the differences in the children themselves, the general influence of the whole of the life of the school upon each child and upon the class units, the attitude of the home to education and teachers in general, the success or failure in school work, the kind of incentives which the teacher puts before his class and the esteem in which the school is held by the people of the neighbourhood in any case. Most of this data falls in the borderland territory of social psychology. But the important contribution which a strictly sociological view of the school and the classroom can make is that it brings the group, both teacher and pupils, into a focus so that justice can be done to the part which each plays and to the formal structure, which provides the canvas upon which the human relationships are sketched in.

XIV

Sociology for the Educator and the Sociology of Education*

A CURRICULUM should no longer be a collection of innumerable haphazard arrangements of the past nor the result of bargaining and compromise between departments whose only aim is to expand like imperialist Balkan states at the expense of their neighbours. A real curriculum is not the result of a battle fought out above the heads of students leaving them finally with a plethora of unco-ordinated knowledge. Real curriculum-making is a most responsible business because on its success will depend which topics from the storehouse of knowledge and culture will survive and which dynamic ideas will be presented for transmission to future generations.

Conscious of this social, cultural and political significance of a curriculum, the drafters no longer start from the idea 'knowledge, more knowledge' but rather to quote the title of a book published in 1939 by R. S. Lynd, *Knowledge for What?*[1] The purposes which guide us will show us what ought to be taught and how much of it ought to be taught and where and how one subject links with another. You may compare a real curriculum to a musical score written for a large orchestra. Such music is never a compromise between competing instruments and neither is a curriculum a competition of solo parts.

There is at least one educational issue on which we now

* This chapter is based upon a lecture given by Professor Mannheim to a conference under the title *Sociology and Education* organized by the Institute of Sociology at Oxford in 1943.

11   143

tend to agree and this is that democracy will not survive unless the citizens fundamentally agree on the main outline of the social order and the values for which the nation stands. This sympathy and agreement can be brought about on a purely emotional level but also on a level where intelligence and judgment play their part. In the past in England habit-making and unconscious solidarity have played a large part. In Fascist countries inculcation of attitudes through propaganda and drill may work but in a modern democracy solidarity with one's country is only possible if the citizen is capable of judging the issues on which he is called to make decisions and this power of discrimination in its turn depends upon a proper appraisal of social relations.

What does the training college candidate want to know of society, and to achieve this purpose what does he need to know of sociology? He asks the sociologist to give him the tools of sociological analysis, to sketch for him the groundwork of this approach to knowledge. He wants to know the elementary social processes from which the more complex ones are built up and he wants to become acquainted with those basic concepts without which no rational analysis of social phenomena is feasible. The student thinks that the sociologist can help him to understand some of the main causes of the social, economic and spiritual crisis, indeed the crisis of democracy itself. If he understands these things as a citizen and as a beginner in sociology, he can turn them to good account when he comes to teach future generations in a developing democracy.

The student in training is aware that he has to think about the place of education in the social order. He wishes to co-ordinate the work which he does with the influences which come through the child from the family, the community, the church, the factory and through the social work agencies. Therefore he is bound to try to understand the sociological nature of these institutions so that he may assess their educational contribution.

We are coming to recognize that the sociological method of analysis can provide us with a number of valuable insights if it is directed to the situations and issues peculiar to the profession of teaching and from all that has been said in the preceding paragraph it is apparent that those who are prepared to teach have as educators to become familiar with what sociology is and what it aims to do.

I. SOCIOLOGY FOR THE EDUCATOR

(a) *Human nature and the social order*

We shall need to consider here how far human nature can be moulded by society and obviously psychological knowledge will be of the greatest importance. What do we know about instincts and habits and how these are related to and productive of a culture? As we have seen earlier in this book the concept of conditioning, deconditioning and reconditioning is an important contribution to the understanding of learning and obviously plays a part in all that we understand by education. If we go back to the beginning of a person's life we can see how a society works upon him and indeed how different societies produce different patterns of behaviour. The contacts of infants with their mothers, the elementary processes of co-operation, conflict, accommodation, assimilation and isolation are all important in helping to form the rudiments of personality. One of the most important is conflict, where there is a clash of opinion or behaviour either between individuals or groups and it is very important in any society to understand for what reasons these conflicts have come into being, and how the society has learned to deal with them because in the discussion of problems like these we come to understand the dilemmas which are often presented to us which force us to choose. These are essentially moral problems arising from human relationships and show us how individuals learn to live with each other and what are the healthy or distorted relationships that can grow up.

It is one thing to be dealing with individuals who are members of a primary group and who come into personal contact with one another. It is a different matter to deal with groups and the social forces which they create and in terms of which they have to make their judgments. Individual competition is not at all the same thing as group competition even though they may very often be made to serve similar purposes. The team spirit is not simply the individual desire to triumph in each member multiplied by the number in the team; it has a more complex reality than this and it is valuable for the educator to understand it.

I mentioned above the importance of beginning to understand the necessity for choices and the bases for the act of choosing. Besides the conflicts for which we can find a solution, we have to realize that there is always the possibility in any society of individual or social disorganization or breakdown. Aggressiveness may itself be a symptom of fear, it certainly begets fear in many other people and is a potent cause of anxiety and misery. But it is not always the deliberate attempts to seek for self-aggrandisement or domination which cause breakdown or disorganization in a society. Very often when the habits or ways of thinking in a society are at a transitional stage we find many examples of confusion and disturbance. Two excellent instances may be found in the Reformation which was not only a theological movement but a naissance in science and politics as well as a renaissance in philosophy and literature. The second example can be found in Germany after the first World War where the old power groups in the Junkers and officers of the army gave place to an anarchy of disenchantment and liberal optimism. Here was a democracy trying to take root in a soil far too shallow for it, where the groups knew how to disagree on liberal grounds but had very little idea of how to fill the void of German nationalism with some uniting policy. The transitional stage between late German feudalism and the anarchism of the twenties gave Hitler and the Nazis their chance. By disjointing the various interested groups and trying to give them some sense of common purpose in a destiny which the Master Race was supposed to achieve, Hitler divided and ruled. As a piece of sustained and ruthless political opportunism his policies will deserve the attention of history as a variation on the theme of pragmatism in politics which modulated into a dominant mystique.

The people who belong to a society can only be relatively happy and secure in it if they feel that the kind of values for which it stands and the demands which it makes upon its members are acceptable. Economic security helps in this, the feeling that there is work to do and that the labourer is worthy of his hire. Similarly the sense of a long and continuous history perpetuated in many picturesque and meaningful traditions provides for many British people a psychological security which is all the stronger for being very largely unconscious and unexamined so that when its strength does appear in times of crisis it surprises those who expect loyalty to be associated with an articulated set of principles rather than a time-worn and flexible set of social institutions. Durkheim, the brilliant French sociologist, tried to show that the integration of a community in terms of its values and its norms of behaviour can be indicated by the suicide rate in that group. Durkheim maintained that the suicide rate is the function of the degree of integration of the group and that a state of affairs can arise which might be called normlessness (*anomie*) in which rapid changes or crises have so shaken the cohesion of a society that it is powerless to offer standards or norms to which its members can aspire. Thus when the stockmarket crashes the financier is adrift and uncomprehending; when the disillusionment of coming defeat saps the soldier's confidence in the power of his generals to lead; when unemployment leaves men aimless and listless as the submerged and forgotten fraction—these are examples of the beginnings of *anomie*. When the disintegration spreads widely through the nation as happened at the fall of the Roman Empire after the barbarian invasions, then that civilization disappears in its former style from history to reappear later after the stubborn human fashion in some different guise.[2]

In our society we have various forms of control, various means of guaranteeing some kind of justice and the most obvious of these is the law, whose main responsibility is to see that brute strength and ruthlessness are curbed in the interests of equity. The educator should understand the forces which make for control in a society because if he considers these closely he will have to consider the nature of freedom and the acceptable forms in which to express it. Rousseau and others have asked if it is possible to compel men to be free and the educator ought at some point to ask himself if he can justify the law which compels men to be educated, or at any rate schooled.

Besides the formal expression of law there are many other sanctions and controls within a society, ranging from customs and conventions to what are often called differentials in financial reward. The educator understands the society for which he is helping to prepare his pupils better if he sees the relationships between freedom, authority, discipline and control.

Both the sociologist and the psychologist have much to say on the theme of valuation. If we regard valuation as a judgment and justification of choice we can at once see that it is important to know what we choose and how we mobilize our ideas and our feelings to justify the choice. Similarly it would be helpful to understand in what ways society recommends and supports certain standards for our acceptance. Take for instance the present position of the so-called working classes and compare them with the standing and power of the serfs in feudal times. To take another example, the position of women in our day is vastly different in this country from what it was even half a century ago. How has it come about and what are the agencies by which the transformation in public opinion has been effected? So that new value systems can be passed on in the common currency it is important for educators to understand something of these processes and particularly to realize that within the same culture there can exist a number of different value systems in the various sub-cultures.

One of the most powerful social stimuli is the achievement of status in society. It helps to enhance self-esteem through the gaining of power and the recognition of authority with the privileges attendant upon it. A career is on the one hand a social phenomenon and on the other it is a pattern around which many people organize their lives. Money is often a sign of success in this way; school, degree of education, profession —these are all criteria which help to give status in various forms, and here again the educator should be aware of the various resources in society for according prestige and leadership.

(*b*) *The impact of social groups upon the individual. Why do groups form and what are their characteristics?*

In our society no one can escape being born into a family, living in a house in a neighbourhood, taking part in play groups, going to school, and probably to church, perhaps joining one or other of the voluntary associations like the Scouts or the Guides and so on. We have already discussed earlier in this book the relationship between the family and the society in which it is set. Obviously it is important for any educator to have some means of detecting the ways in which a community can be an educational agency. There are in existence a number of environmental studies which take into account the conditions of the home and the neighbourhood and the organization of societies and groups to which various members of the family belong, the resources of entertainment in the neighbourhood and the habits people adopt in spending their leisure. We are aware of the tendency to move educational responsibility away from the family into the hands of the institutions and the experts who work in them. The educator must be prepared to think about the whole issue of the relationship between the responsibilities of the school and the other resources in the neighbourhood and the community and the contributions which each can make.

One of the most important problems of valuation is the assumed dichotomy between work and leisure. The change from handicraft to industry has had profound effects upon the nature of the work done and the working incentives. In accompaniment with this, the transition from the old communal ways of spending leisure to mass enjoyment has led to the setting up of what we might call institutions for the enjoyment of free time. Leisure in the machine age has become commercialized and circumscribed by habit. There is far less spontaneous creativeness in leisure while it is freely admitted that the standards of opportunities offered, for instance, for the enjoyment of music or the drama, are potentially far greater than they have ever been.

We have always been aware of culture as a word used to signify a special kind of behaviour and knowledge. We are now faced with the question of the continuity of culture on different levels of society. Have we any notion in these days of the transformations which are taking place towards a mass culture and is there indeed any sense in this phrase?

(c) Social structure

The state is an organization to which we frequently refer and which needs a good deal of clarification. One of its purposes is to indicate the limits within which we ought to behave to one another as individuals and within which one grouping or nation should behave towards others. The state can only undertake its responsibilities with our consent, since it is essentially man-made and maintains itself with our approval because men are the life blood of its existence. It is in fact a necessary legal and political fiction. From the point of view of organization it has both legislative and executive responsibilities and through its institutions it gives to its officers the responsibility of formulating agreed ways of acting and defining the instruments of control as between groups and within the groups. The instruments by which the state acts are authority and power and the channels through which these are directed we call institutions. In a democracy the final political control is in the hands of the people but this is an ambiguous and perhaps misleading notion because there are many interested groups which seek to influence the judgment of the voter and in a sense necessarily so. A large-scale democracy could not work unless there was some kind of group organization such as the political parties. Yet the very existence of the parties means that many voters who do not find any one of the parties representing their points of view have to choose the one which comes nearest to representing their policies.

The act of handing over a great deal of our political responsibility to a parliament takes away from us the right to decide many issues and one of the principal problems of the existence of the state in a democratic society is the degree of freedom which it permits to the individual voter in matters of personal and political significance. Obviously in a country run on Marxist or Fascist lines this problem is greatly simplified. An educator must understand the state as an organization which lays down many of the lines within which he and other citizens may work. While it has a theoretical basis for its organization, an account which may be given in terms of political and moral philosophy, it also has a superstructure of administration. In any state the relationship between the institution of parliament, the permanent Civil Service, the armed forces and the police are of the greatest significance because they indicate the kind of freedom which prevails in the lives of ordinary people from day to day. The educator must understand the state in its working as a frame-group.

The economics of a society can be pretty clearly seen in the class structure and conflict and the importance attached to the various forms of property control. Marx laid down that one of the ways of exerting power in society was to own the means of production and in the kind of society to which he looked forward, the state was to own and administer these in the interests of the people. In a capitalist or mixed economy ownership is in the hands of individuals or groups of individuals and educators have to understand the motivations to which these different points of view give rise, because they will help to establish the attitudes of parents and children and of the teachers themselves, to the institution of school.

Sociology for the educator must confront him with the main working mechanisms of a society. He must be aware of the difference between revolution and reform, he must be able to see that democracy operates on the basis of agreed change and that this is not at all the method of a totalitarian state. A democracy must set up institutions which will permit a tolerance of conflict and doubt while at the same time ensuring an even more deeply held conviction of the right to freedom as far as possible. Perhaps the most difficult thing to see in our society is that changes are being brought about not only by deliberate political action or compromise but by cultural influences of all kinds ranging from education in our schools and universities to the advertisements on our hoardings and the effect on our way of life of technical inventions.

I would maintain that in these days the educator must be sensitized by the study of sociology to the structure of the social order in which he lives, the obvious or concealed impact of social groups upon him, and the relationship between persons and the social order in which they are set.

II. THE SOCIOLOGY OF EDUCATION

The school is only one agency in society concerned with education. It takes its place with the home, the industrial order, the church, the voluntary agencies, the social services, the mass media. We can draw a fairly useful distinction between formal and informal education, but we should recognize that while we give the school a place of great importance which it deserves, the total effect of education is not to be found only through the formal agencies. Indeed, part of the responsibility of the school will be to enable its pupils to detect more and more of the informal influences which are flitting incessantly but quickly through their field of consciousness.

We have long been familiar with the idea that an historical survey of the development of educational ideas in western Europe begins with Greek society and over a period of two thousand years becomes transformed both in its aims and its ideals. As the aims and ideals have transformed themselves so too have the methods. At seven the Greek boy learned the alphabet by rote and then he was set to write the letters on wax tablets. He progressed to two- or three-letter syllables and then to simple words, but not necessarily words which were used. This rote method has been used in one form or another for many centuries and knowledge has been built up in this cumulative and additive way. The project method and learning from experience, the recent trends towards the integration of knowledge by jumping the barriers of subjects—these have encouraged the initiative of the learner and enlivened the whole business.

Institutions of education have exerted a considerable influence in the past and the present because they have set up and controlled professional standards and during the period of compulsory education have had a great deal to do with the creation of the social type. Not that there is one kind of person produced by the schools—indeed the criticism of the public schools in the nineteenth century was that while they produced a recognizable kind of boy with widely admitted virtues and defects, they were supposed also to produce a caste which was separated off from the common run of men.

It would be a valuable exercise for all educators to try to trace the changes which have taken place in the position of the public schools and the universities in our society. They could then see how apparently the same institution can serve completely different purposes at different periods in history.

While the school exists to serve the society by preparing young people in accepted ways it also has to help in the task of social selection, using this term in a strictly neutral sense and without any overtones of privilege. The schools do not earn their esteem in the society to which they belong simply by their own efforts, important though these are. Very often they gain prestige because they prepare for careers which are much sought after and for which other schools do not prepare. To put it another way the standing of a school is in part decided by the openings to careers which it can offer, hence its selective function is not simply an intellectual matter by which pupils of a similar level of ability are brought together in one school, it is also a social and economic matter. To illustrate this, all educators should examine closely and in detail what is meant by the phrase 'parity of esteem' and it will be seen that no matter how splendid the buildings and equipment of a school may be, these are not the main criteria by which it gains its reputation. We should have to consider the number of years which pupils commonly spend in the school; the qualifications and the training of the staff; the variety of courses provided in the school; the kind of jobs which the pupils take—and so on. If we looked at our educational institutions in this way, and even more if we compared them with the practice of other countries, we should be able to write some very valuable chapters of social history.

III. THE SOCIOLOGY OF TEACHING

If we go inside a school and try to see how it works we shall find that the curriculum is only one of the factors which we must take into consideration. The assumptions which the headmaster and his staff make about the stage of development of the children in their care and their views on what they want them to think of the curriculum that has been put before them will influence very greatly whether the pupils are docile under the teaching of authorities, or critical in the common exploration of a topic. In any school we shall find evidence of relationships with the world outside and the extent and kind of these are very important.

The life of the school is very often lived outside the classroom, and in the ceremonies and games the school is able to express the degree of collective effort and self-awareness which exist. Similarly in the teacher-pupil relationship a great deal can be told about the psychological climate of the school. Should the teacher be a friend, a comrade, a leader, an authority or a combination of these? What degree of social distance exists between the teacher and his pupils? If there is an open or concealed conflict between the teacher and his class the quality of the learning and the feeling in the community are likely to be quite different from that to be found in a school where the common purpose is evident in the amity which exists.

There is of course a rich literature on the stereotyped responses of teachers and it is to be expected that a figure of authority who has been known in one form or another to pretty well everyone living in a society is likely to give rise to many public commentaries expressed in the simplified form of cartoons, legends, stereotypes or anecdotes.

The parts played by the teacher at various periods of a pupil's life ranging from infancy to near adulthood are bound to be very various. If he is a few years older than his sixth formers he stands in a very different relationship to them from the elderly spinster teaching her class of infants. It is salutary and necessary for educators to take a long and close look at the occupational roles which the teacher plays both in relation to the organization of the school and to the life-view of the teacher himself as he grows older. Youth, middle life and old age have varying forms of response in teaching as in all other professions, and the educator must be prepared to face and interpret these facts. Similarly he will find in the school an administrative organization which also needs to be understood, because the different part which the administrator plays can best be understood if it is put in its place in the total educational enterprise alongside that of the teacher.[3]

IV. CONCLUSION

These remarks on a curriculum of sociology for the educator, and the sociology of education are partly too comprehensive and partly too limited. If we look at the outline suggested we see that from the point of view of a complete training in sociology it is quite inadequate, but it is likely to be much too comprehensive for the student who has not been prepared in sociological ideas and who has only a limited time to spend on them. From the topics which have been suggested those could be selected which provide the right combination for any particular student, but once the topics have been chosen and delimited, detailed and careful development of them is essential because at present there is a danger that untrained people will overnight call themselves 'sociologists of education' and by their dilettantism spoil the reputation both of the subject and of the profession of educator.

Very much depends in the future on the reputation of the educator in society. In a bygone age the bankers were the respectable people. In a democratically-planned society the teachers will have to play one of the noblest parts. This they can only achieve by regarding their work as a serious attempt to understand and to contribute to the life of the community.

PART FIVE

CONCLUSION

XV

The Future

No educational activity or research is adequate in the present stage of consciousness unless it is conceived in terms of a sociology of education. Apart from the philosophical, psychological and technical approaches, we are gradually becoming aware of the significance of the social context in which education works, and this very awareness produces new insight at every stage. This need for the sociological approach to education is due to the very simple fact that tradition is fading in the most important spheres of life. In an age of tradition, education was simply one of the unconscious techniques for assisting the infant to grow up into a given social order. The more these silent means of transmission lose their effect, however, the more they have to be replaced by conscious processes, and these in their turn only improve along with an awareness of the circumstances in which they are expected to operate. In many spheres of life we can no longer rely upon the spontaneous emanation of a tradition; the main changes taking place do so too quickly to make spontaneous adjustment and unconscious selection reliable.

The principal contribution of the sociological approach to the history and the theory of education is to draw attention to the fact that neither educational aims nor educational techniques can be conceived without a context, but rather, that they are to a very large extent socially directed. Who teaches whom for what society, when and how, as the sociological questions were once framed.

This continual process of referring values and techniques to the social context, if rightly understood, does not contradict an absolutist or a Christian view. The eternal core of the gospel, it seems to me, cannot consist in a dogmatic fixation on the specific setting in which truth appeared at that time. Its historical comprehension can only consist in a continuous re-interpretation of its deeper meaning. This is the only way of bringing to a synthesis the eschatological and the historical elements in Christianity, which has always been one of its main themes. At the same time, this is also the only way of maintaining that healthy distance which is the result of belief in the transcendental, from the ephemeral in worldly affairs, without losing the sense of and an interest in reality.

Our investigation into the sociological foundations of education cannot be a purely academic one, piling up facts for their own sake. There is something definite we want to know. We are in search of something which should never be lost sight of in our research. We want to understand our time, the predicament of this age and what healthy education could contribute to a regeneration of society and man. In this quest for orientation sociology is a tool and we shall use it in a two-fold sense: as a special theory of education and as a new approach to its history. These two means of access will continually draw upon each other. We shall study history in order to have a broader background to the understanding of our own society, but this study of history will be intensified by our desire to be able ultimately to build up a sociological theory of education which can assist us in our present task.

As I formerly indicated, the sociological approach looks at education not as an aim in itself but as a part of the social-historical dynamics and of the *Weltanschauung* which corresponds to it. If it is true that the child is never educated in the abstract, but, rather, for a given society, then it must be possible for the sociologist to interpret the educational aims of an epoch from the needs and ultimate strivings of that very same society. But it would lead us too far afield to collect all the possible aims which developed in history and it will therefore perhaps be helpful to describe a few main types which could be used as a measuring rod in our historical researches. In this connection I should like to draw attention to the classification of educational aims by Max Weber. He distinguishes three main types of education throughout history. The first he calls charis-

160

matic education, the second, education aiming at culture, and the third, specialist education.

Charismatic education is dominant in the magical period or in periods in which religion reaches its highest point. In the first case it wants to arouse hidden powers latent in man, in the second to awaken religious intuition and the inner readiness for transcendental experience. In both cases the predominant aim is not the transfer of specific content or skill but to stir up certain innate powers which are, if not superhuman, at least the limited possession of the chosen.

Highly different from charismatic education is *education for culture*. Here the belief is that certain contents perceived as classical have the inner qualifications of breeding a certain social type. It is not only the substance which is valued but the style of life which unconsciously will be transferred through the ideas presented. Not the content as such but its formative educational power is being stressed. Good examples are the creation of the gentleman or of the Chinese mandarin who acquire through a study of the classics a certain mental mood, style of thought, and inner disposition and sentiment. It cannot be denied that, up to the present, the various forms of humanism have had the function of creating social distinction, and the way of life instilled by them could only be followed by some privileged classes who had the leisure and surplus energy for cultivation. The real sociological question of humanism in our age is whether its values can be transferred from the so-called leisured classes to lower-middle and working classes.[1]

Specialist education seeks to transfer a special knowledge or skill and is strictly correlated with the growth of division of labour which makes the specialist indispensable in modern industrial society. This education loses sight both of the deeper levels of the self which were the main concern of religious education and of the humanistic many-sidedness of personality which was still the ideal of the educated few. Although it produces the necessary cogs and wheels in the social machine specialist education disintegrates both the personality and the mental powers for understanding the human situation which has to be mastered.

A thorough-going study of the social origins, the special methods of putting these three educational ideals into practice, will help us to interpret our present situation and will lead to decisions as to whether each of these techniques could be used in different compartments of life, and in different stages of the individual's development. Because these three different types of education, although they developed in a detectable sequence in history, are not mutually exclusive, but rather complement each other, a continuous awareness of their special significance could enable us to establish their proper place in modern education.

Not only the content of education, its ideals and its ultimate aims, vary from one society to another, but also many of the seemingly universal qualities of man, sometimes even quite imponderable forms of experience, change with the changing *Weltanschauung*. This rather subtle sphere of the changing forms of experience in the world, *die Erlebnisformen*, to use the German expression, is a theme in itself. The transfer of these changing forms of experience occurs through invisible channels in face-to-face contacts, but they help to determine the way in which people will react spontaneously to both the trivial and the important objectives of life. Whether they will shrink from cruelty, whether they will rather choose the way of withdrawal within themselves, or fight out their case, whether they will neglect action because they exhaust their power on the level of verbalism and rhetoric, whether they will be ascetic or strive for self-expression, whether different forms of love and sentiment will predominate in their interpersonal relations or whether they will rather indulge in creating barriers and distance, all largely depends on the examples presented in their surroundings.

Although it appears as if these changing attitudes and minute forms of experience were either innate or produced by spontaneous and unconscious processes of the invisible social texture, even in the past, when there was less theoretical awareness of educational aims than there is today, much care has been given to their procreation. In our society the symptoms of re-barbarization are perhaps largely due to the neglect of the cultivation of these human attitudes and sentiments or to the fact that they have been left without control. This negligence on the part of official education in a society in which the family and the community are losing their educational power, ultimately means that the creation of basic attitudes is left to vulgarizing agencies such as the cinema, television, radio, press, which satisfy the thirst of the masses for basic attitudes and new forms of experience.

Within the framework of the study of basic attitudes we must of necessity consider the history of fundamental virtues. Some of these are undoubtedly widespread in the world, and this corresponds to the fact that in traditional society the primary groups, like the family, the neighbourhood and the community, will always develop the very same primary virtues, such as love and mutual help. But apart from these basic virtues there are some equally elementary virtues which vary with society. Courage, for instance, or piety, are not acknowledged to the same degree in all societies. It is characteristic that in China when a general pacification took place the virtue of heroism was rejected by Confucius and that, in history, the changing significance of piety very much depends on the changing role which the various generations play in different societies. In the same way, restraint and dignity are virtues which are chiefly linked up with the existence of some leading élites to whom self-control has become a basic virtue. The moderation of medieval chivalry is another instance of such a basic virtue bound to time and class. Rhetorical eloquence is a virtue of the market place and of democratic societies, but history very often produces shades and combinations of such basic virtues, such as the Jesuits' ideal of the *sapiens et eloquens pietas*.

The significance of a study of these basic virtues in their genuine historical context consists in helping us to re-establish some of them and to find new ones which conform to our age. Since we are at last becoming aware that their function is to create that minimum of social conformity without which no society can continue, such a study may reveal to us why these basic virtues disintegrate in the present stage of capitalism. Perhaps it would also show us the educational techniques by which they could be maintained or developed, directly or indirectly.

But not only can the attitudes and the basic virtues, these atoms of any *Weltanschauung*, be studied in the social context; even the more comprehensive patterns of life, are subject to change and are the perceptible expression of the ultimate

163

strivings of a society. Only in a society like our own could the idea of fate and life history degenerate into the bureaucratic idea of a life career. In place of this idea there were, in more meaningful times, the visible symbols of different ways of life. The sage of antiquity, the saint, the monk, the heretic, the martyr, the ascetic in religious culture, the knight in chivalry, *l'honnête homme* and *l'homme vertueux et sensible* in later periods, were all educational patterns integrating life histories.

We should not be completely blind to some recent trends which work towards the creation of acceptable patterns of living. The youth movement has undoubtedly produced some of the new ideals of the sincere man who wants to find a genuine relation to nature and to his fellow beings. Psychoanalysis is striving towards a life pattern the ideal of which is to gain a new sense of reality and to escape the distortion created by uncontrolled repressions, fears and anxieties. In the English ideal of never over-stating facts, there is a treasure of self-control, and appreciation of common sense; in the stakhanovite worker of the Russians is to be found the ideal of the pioneer ready to make people efficient, enthusiastic and willing to sacrifice for the community.

Another aspect of a sociological study of education is the problem of synthesizing different trends operating in different social layers and in different ethnological and geographical regions. In periods of high culture there was a partly conscious, partly unconscious balance created between the contributions of the different groups to education. This balance was sometimes based upon the idea of a hierarchy of separated estates or castes, each one of which produced its own cultural contribution on different levels. In medieval society, for instance, the very same religious influence was experienced by the peasants on a different mental level from that experienced in the growing cities of the time. The erudite man and the cleric experienced it on a more intellectual level, the product of which was rational theology; the knight in terms of action and worldly practice. The democratic conception adds to the idea of synthesis the free intercommunication between social layers and their cultural contributions. Its main concern is the access of the gifted members of the lower classes to the élites, the invention of right methods of social selection, and the preservation of society from deteriorating into undifferentiated masses. Its cultural balance is based upon processes more complex than and even antagonistic to segregation and careful isolation of the groups.

Another aspect of synthesizing the different forces operating in a culture consists in harmonizing antagonistic elements, for instance the contrasts between the school and life, work and leisure, action and reflection, self-control and self-expression, individualization and co-operation, change and tradition. Such studies are equally instructive, both when they deal with periods in which a balance has been reached and with periods in which disharmony and destruction follow. For instance, the study of the consequences of the industrial revolution, which has been the main agency in upsetting the balance of modern society, is still very significant and here we can learn a great deal from the criticisms developed by men like Kingsley, Morris and Ruskin and later by the Socialists.

When approaching the study of our age we shall have to aim at a general sociological diagnosis able to explain the main educational problems in terms of more fundamental structural changes operating in our society. We are living in an age of planning which is bound to find a new form of co-ordination, we are living in an age in which the forces of both tradition and enlightenment are disintegrating, we are living in an age which passes from the stage of the predominance of limited élites to mass democracy, we are living in an age whose uncontrolled forces bring about dehumanization and disintegration of the personality. Ultimately education has to be conceived of as a new form of social control which is neither the inculcation of Fascism nor the complete anarchy of a deteriorated *laisser-faire* policy.

But all these studies of the historical background of education will be exclusively directed to a better understanding of our immediate task. The number of historical items we will study, and the choice of them, will depend on the means available, and on the practical issues that seem to be most urgent. Perhaps it would be useful to mention some of those immediate practical issues on which we will have to take a decision sooner or later, and which will necessarily react upon the historical part of our work.

It may be that our first task will be to decide what the educational aims of modern society should be. It may be that our main interest will be to investigate the existing alterations in the balance between the contributions of the home, church, school, factory, and public life towards moulding individual character. If so, an historical study will have to be supplemented by a survey of the existing educational institutions in this country and their inter-relations, in order to discover the strategic points at which the educational reconstruction ought to begin.

It may be that we will come to the conviction that the cultural decline in our society is mainly due to the disintegration of the leading élites, and that a mass society can only preserve its cultural traditions if, in spite of its democratic basis, it creates a more adequate selection and the right scope for the influence of these élites.

It may be that the crisis of humanistic ideals or of religious life will become the focal point of our interest. Ultimately it may be that the factors making for the disintegration of personality and dehumanization will become central. Then, among others, a study of labour attitudes and the problem of leisure in modern society will have to be stressed.

Thus the next task should perhaps be to select from these scattered suggestions and others those which are the most urgent and promising ones, and gradually to translate them into even more detailed and specialized research schemes. If we make an appropriate choice, I feel that these questions are not too comprehensive. One could show that the right command of primary sources and of the existing literature on the subject already offers answers to a great number of them. At the moment we have to aim at the creation of a pioneering élite among our best teachers, clergymen, youth movement leaders, and anyone who has to do basic work in the field of education, in order to give them an orientation based upon sociological knowledge, in the hope that this will bring more unity and purpose into their action.

Notes

CHAPTER I

[1] See DEWEY, John: *Democracy and Education*. New York, Macmillan Co., 1916, p. 144,
    and HORNE, H. H.: *The Democratic Philosophy of Education*. New York, Macmillan Co., 1932.
[2] PAINTER, F. V. N.: *Luther on Education*. Philadelphia, Lutheran Publication Society, 1899.
[3] Making a rough comparison using data from *Education in 1958* (Cmnd. 777) and *Returns from Universities and University Colleges 1958-59* (Cmnd. 1166) it appears that of over 830,000 children between 10 and 11 years of age, about 14 to 15 per cent. went to selective secondary schools in 1958. Of the 18-year-old age group of roughly 572,000, over 22,000 went to universities in England and Wales for the first time in 1958. This represents roughly 4 per cent. of the age group.
[4] See CLARKE, Sir Fred: *The Study of Education in England*. London, Oxford University Press, 1943,
    and HOCKING, W. E.: *Man and State*. New Haven, Yale University Press, 1926.
    In his book: *Freedom in the Educative Society*, Sir Fred CLARKE has collected his ideas as well as those of W. E. HOCKING on this problem. He has dedicated this book (published by the University of London Press in 1948) to the memory of Karl Mannheim.
[5] ADAMS, Sir John: *The Evolution of Educational Theory*. London, Macmillan, 1912.

CHAPTER II

[1] On the work of David STOW see CURTIS, S. J.: *History of Education in Great Britain*. London, University Tutorial Press, Ltd., 1948, as well as STOW, David: *The Training System*. Glasgow, 1840.
[2] See ADAMS, Sir John, op. cit. (note 5 in Chapter I).
[3] For DILTHEY see *Dilthey, Wilhelm: Selected Readings from His Works and an Introduction to His Sociological and Philosophical Work*, by H. A. Hodges. London, Routledge and Kegan Paul, 1952.
[4] MILL, J. S.: 'Inaugural Address at St. Andrews,' published in CAVENAGH, F. A.: *James and John Stuart Mill, on Education*. Cambridge Univ. Press, 1931, pp. 132–198.

CHAPTER III

[1] DEWEY, John: *The School and Society*. Revised ed. Chicago, 1916.
See further Sir Fred Clarke, op. cit. (note 4 in Chapter I).
[2] VEBLEN, Th.: *The Theory of the Leisure Class*. New York, Macmillan Co., 1912.
[3] JAMES, William: *Talks to Teachers on Psychology*. London, Longmans, Green & Co., 1899.
[4] BAUDOUIN, C.: *Suggestion and Autosuggestion*. London, Allen & Unwin, 1920.
[5] FREUD, S.: *Introductory Lectures on Psycho-Analysis*. London, Allen and Unwin, 1923.
FREUD, S.: *New Introductory Lectures on Psychoanalysis*. New York, Norton, 1933; London, Hogarth Press, 1935.
[6] For the HILL brothers see ADAMSON, J. W.: *English Education 1789–1902*. Cambridge University Press, 1930.
On Thomas DAY—a friend of the Edgeworths—see a reference in CURTIS, S. J. and BOULTWOOD, M. E. A.: *A Short History of Educational Ideas*. London, University Tutorial Press, 1953, p. 392.
The Edgeworths (R. L. Edgeworth and his daughter Maria, authors of *Practical Education*), played the role of educational pioneers at the beginning of the 19th century in England.
[7] WHEELER, Olive: *The Adventure of Youth*. University of London Press, 1945, p. 12.
Other books mentioned by Karl MANNHEIM in connection with topics in this chapter are as follows:
FLUGEL, J. C.: *A Hundred Years of Psychology*. London, Duckworth, 1937.
HORNEY, K.: *New Ways in Psychoanalysis*. New York, Norton & Co., 1939.
HORNEY, K.: *The Neurotic Personality of Our Time*. New York, Norton & Co., 1937.
RAZRAN, G. H. S.: 'Conditioned Responses.' A classified bibliography. *Psychological Bulletin*, Vol. 34, 1937, pp. 191–256.
WOODWORTH, R. S.: *Contemporary Schools of Psychology*. New York, The Ronald Press, 1948. (First published in Britain in 1931.)

CHAPTER IV

[1] See LIVINGSTONE, R. W.: *Greek Ideals and Modern Life*. London, Oxford University Press, 1935, and Harvard University Press, Cambridge, Mass.,
and JAEGER, W.: *Paideia—The Ideals of Greek Culture*. 3 vols., Oxford, Blackwell, 1934–36,
as well as ROSS, J. S.: *Groundwork of Educational Theory*. London, Harrap, 1942.
[2] See WILKINS, A.: *Roman Education*. Cambridge University Press, 1921.
as well as GWYNN, A.: *Roman Education from Cicero to Quintilian*. London, Oxford University Press, 1926.

³ See RASHDALL, Hastings: *The Universities of Europe in the Middle Ages.* 3 vols. New edition edited by Sir F. M. Powicke and A. B. Emden, London, Oxford University Press, 1936.

See further ARMYTAGE, W. H. G.: *Civic Universities.* London, Ernest Benn, Ltd., 1955.

⁴ MARTIN, A. V.: *Sociology of the Renaissance.* London, Routledge and Kegan Paul, 1944.

⁵ FROMM, E.: *The Fear of Freedom.* London, Kegan Paul, Trench, Trubner & Co., 1942.

⁶ See MARSHALL, T. H.: 'The Nature and Determinants of Social Status' in *Year Book of Education 1953.* Joint Editors: R. K. Hall, N. Hans, J. A. Lauwerys. London, Evans Bros., 1953, p. 32. On the concept of 'the gentleman' see *ibid.*, pp. 37–41.

⁷ DEFOE, Daniel: *The Compleat English Gentleman.* Ed. by D. Bulbring. London, D. Nutt, 1890.

See further MacEACHRAN, F.: 'The Gentleman Ideal', *The Nineteenth Century*, Vol. CIV, Dec., 1928, pp. 824–35.

and PALMER, A. S.: *The Ideal of a Gentleman.* London, Routledge, 1908.

as well as HUIZINGA, J.: *Homo Ludens.* London, Routledge and Kegan Paul, 1949.

⁸ See FITCH, Sir Joshua: *Thomas and Matthew Arnold.* London, William Heinemann, 1897,

and WHITEHOUSE, J. H.: *The English Public School.* London, Richards, 1919,

also MACK, E. C.: *Public Schools and British Opinion.* 2 vols. Vol. 1: *1780–1860*, London, Methuen, 1938. Vol. 2: *Since 1860*, New York, Columbia Univ. Press, 1941.

⁹ On the problems dealt with by Mannheim in this chapter see further the following works:

CURTIS, S. J.: *History of Education in Great Britain.* London, University Tutorial Press, Ltd., 1948.

CURTIS, S. J. and BOULTWOOD, M. E. A.: *A Short History of Educational Ideas.* London, University Tutorial Press, Ltd., 1953.

LÖWE, Adolf: *The Universities in Transformation.* London, The Sheldon Press, 1940.

RUSK, R.: *The Doctrines of the Great Educators.* London, Macmillan, 1945.

CHAPTER V

¹ NUNN, Sir Percy: *Education: Its Data and First Principles.* London, Edward Arnold, 1930, p. 9.

² DEWEY, John: *Reconstruction in Philosophy.* New York, Henry Holt, 1920, pp. 207–8.

³ See ABBOTT, T. K.: *Kant's Theory of Ethics.* London, Longmans Green, 1909,

and KANT, Immanuel: *Paedagogik.* (*Kant on Education.*) Trans. by A. Churton. London, Kegan Paul, Trench and Trubner, 1899.

CHAPTER VI

[1] MORGAN, T. H.: 'Are Acquired Characteristics Inherited?' *The Yale Review.* Vol. 13; July, 1924.

[2] DEWEY, John: *Human Nature and Conduct.* New York, Holt, 1922, p. 128.

[3] HULL, Clark, L.: 'Conditioning: Outline of a Systematic Theory of Learning.' *Forty-first Yearbook. National Society for the Study of Education.* Part II: *The Psychology of Learning.* Ed. H. B. Henry. Chicago, University of Chicago Press, 1942, pp. 61–95.

[4] PAVLOV, J. P.: *Lectures on Conditioned Reflexes.* London, Oxford University Press, 1927.

[5] See HILGARD, E. R.: *Theories of Learning.* New York, Appleton-Century-Crofts, 1948, p. 11.

[6] WATSON, J. B.: *Behaviorism.* New York, People's Institute Publishing Co., 1924.

[7] See KOHLER, W.: *Gestalt Psychology.* New York, Liveright, 1929,

and KOFFKA, K.: *The Growth of the Mind.* London, Kegan Paul, Trench, Trubner & Co., 1928, as well as KOFFKA, K.: *Principles of Gestalt Psychology.* New York, Harcourt, 1935.

[8] For McDougall see: McDOUGALL, W.: *An Introduction to Social Psychology.* Boston, John W. Luce, 1926,

and McDOUGALL, W.: *An Outline of Psychology.* London, Methuen, 1923.

For Burt see: BURT, C.: *How the Mind Works.* London, Allen & Unwin, 1935,

and BURT, C.: *The Factors of the Mind.* London, University of London Press, 1940.

[9] See HEALEY, W., BRONNER, A. F. and BOWERS, A. M.: *The Structure and Meaning of Psychoanalysis.* New York, Knopf, 1930,

and HEALY, W.: *Personality in Formation and Action.* London, Chapman, 1938.

See also note 5 in Chapter III.

[10] On Erikson see ERIKSON, E. H. *Childhood and Society.* London, Imago. N. d.

On Kardiner see note 2 in Chapter IX.

For H. S. SULLIVAN see MULLAHY, Patrick: *Oedipus—Myth and Complex. A Review of Psychoanalytic Theory,* with an Introduction by Erich FROMM. New York, Hermitage Press, 1948, espec. Chapter 10.

For Karen HORNEY see *ibid.,* Chapter 8, for Erich FROMM see *ibid.,* Chapter 9.

[11] THORNDIKE, E. L.: *Fundamentals of Learning.* New York, Teachers College, Columbia University, 1932,

and THORNDIKE, E. L.: *Human Nature and the Social Order.* New York, Macmillan, 1940,

as well as THORNDIKE, E. L.: *The Psychology of Learning.* New York, Teachers College, Columbia University, 1913.

[12] See GUTHRIE, E. R.: *The Psychology of Learning.* New York, Harper, 1935,

and SMITH, S. and GUTHRIE, E. R.: *General Psychology in Terms of Behavior.* New York, Appleton, 1921,

as well as GUTHRIE, E. R.: *The Psychology of Human Conflict*. New York, Harper, 1938.
[13] SKINNER, Ch. E.: *Educational Psychology*. London, Staples Press, 1936, and SKINNER, Ch. E.: *The Behavior of Organisms*. New York, Appleton-Century, 1938.
[14] DOLLARD, J. and MILLER, N. E.: *Frustration and Aggression*. New Haven, Yale University Press, 1939.
[15] ALLPORT, G. W.: *Personality. A Psychological Interpretation*. New York, Henry Holt, 1937.
[16] See WOODWORTH, R. S.: *Dynamic Psychology*. New York, Columbia University Press, 1918,
and WOODWORTH, R. S.: *Experimental Psychology*, New York, Holt, 1938.

CHAPTER VII

[1] See note 3 and note 9 in Chapter VI.
[2] MEAD, G. H.: *Mind, Self and Society*. Chicago, University of Chicago Press, 1934.
[3] Other books mentioned by Karl MANNHEIM in connection with topics in this chapter are as follows:
BAGLEY, W. C.: *Determinism in Education*. Baltimore, Warwick and York, 1925,
and BAGLEY, W. C.: *The Educative Process*. London, Macmillan, 1923,
as well as BAGLEY, W. C.: *Educational Values*. New York, Macmillan, 1911.
See also DASHIELL, J. F.: 'A Survey and Synthesis of Learning Theories.' *Psychological Bulletin* (American Psychological Bulletin), Vol. 32, 1935, pp. 261–275.
See further DOLLARD, J. and MILLER, N. E.: *Social Learning and Imitation*, New Haven, Yale University Press, 1941.
See further JENNINGS, H. S., WATSON, J. B., MEYER, A. and THOMAS, W. I.: *Suggestions of Modern Science Concerning Education*. New York, Macmillan Co., 1917. Reissued 1946.
For the contribution of Thomas, W. I., see *ibid.*, pp. 159–197: 'The Persistence of Primary Group Norms in Present day Society, and their Influence in our Educational System.'
McCONNELL, T. R. (*et al.*): 'The Psychology of Learning' in the *Forty-first Yearbook, National Society for the Study of Education*. Part II: *The Psychology of Learning*. Chicago, The University of Chicago Press, 1942.
See further MURPHY, G., MURPHY, L. B. and NEWCOMB, T.: *Experimental Social Psychology*. New York, Harper, 1937,
as well as THOMAS, W. I. and THOMAS, D. S.: *The Child in America*. New York, Knopf, 1928,
and THOMAS, W. I.: *The Unadjusted Girl*. Boston, Little, Brown & Co., 1920,
and finally THOMAS, W. I.: *The Behavior Pattern and the Situation*. Northampton, Mass., Publications of the American Sociological Society, 1928, 1–3.

CHAPTER VIII

[1] See ICHHEISER, G.: 'Zur Psychologie des Nichtkönnens', Engelmann's *Archiv für die Gesamte Psychologie*. Leipzig. Vol. 92, 1934,
and JACOBY, Heinrich: 'Die Befreiung der Schöpferischen Kräfte dargestellt am Beispiele der Musik.' Sonderdruck aus: *Das Werdende Zeitalter*. 4. Jg. 4. Heft. Gotha, Kotz, 1925,
as well as JACOBY, Heinrich: *Jenseits von Musikalisch und Unmusikalisch*. Stuttgart, Enke, 1925,
further AICHHORN, A.: *Wayward Youth*. London, Putnam, 1936. (Original German title: *Verwahrloste Jugend*.) For a more strictly psychoanalytic treatment see
LANDAUER, K.: 'Intellektuelle Hemmungen'. Zeitschrift für *Psychoanalytische Padagogik*. No. 11-12, 1930.

[2] ADLER, Alfred: *Understanding Human Nature*. London, George Allen & Unwin, 1930.

[3] FENICHEL, Otto: *The Psychoanalytic Theory of Neuroses*. New York, Norton & Co. 1945.

[4] See SCHONELL, F. J.: *Backwardness in the Basic Subjects*. Edinburgh, Oliver & Boyd, 1942,
and BURT, C.: *The Backward Child*. University of London Press, 1937,
as well as BURT, C.: *The Subnormal Mind*. London, Oxford University Press, 1935,
see further BURT, C. *The Factors of the Mind. An Introduction to the Factor Analysis in Psychology*. London, University of London Press, 1940.

[5] BURLINGHAM, D., and FREUD, Anna: *Infants Without Families*. London, Allen and Unwin, 1946.

CHAPTER IX

[1] PLATO: *The Republic*. Translated with an Introduction by A. D. Lindsay. London, Dent, 1935, Book VII.

[2] See LINTON, R.: *The Study of Man*. New York, Appleton-Century Crofts, 1936,
and KARDINER, A.: *The Psychological Frontiers of Society*. New York, Columbia University Press, 1945,
see also KARDINER, A.: *The Individual and His Society* with a Foreword and two anthropological reports by R. LINTON. New York, Columbia University Press, 1939.

[3] COOLEY, C. H.: *Human Nature and the Social Order*. New York, Scribner, 1928.

[4] PIAGET, J.: *The Language and Thought of the Child*. London, Kegan Paul, 1926.

[5] See ISAACS, Susan: *The Intellectual Growth in Young Children*. London, Routledge, 1930.

[6] MORENO, J. L.: *Who Shall Survive?* New York, Nervous Diseases Publishing Co., 1934.

[7] For William JAMES see Note 3 in Chapter III above.

8 For G. H. MEAD see Note 2 in Chapter VII above.
9 HARTSHORNE, H. and MAY, M. A.: *Studies in Deceit.* New York, Macmillan Co., 1938.
10 RANK, Otto: *Beyond Psychology.* New York, Dover Printing Co., 1941.

CHAPTER X

1 See JACOBY's studies on the problems of musical education above: Note 1 Chapter VIII.
2 MORENO, J. L.: *Psychodrama.* Vol. I. New York, Beacon House, 1946.
3 DEWEY, John: *The School and Society.* University of Chicago Press, 1916, p. 90.

CHAPTER XI

1 On these problems see WEBER, Max: *The Protestant Ethic and the Spirit of Capitalism.* (Translated by Talcott Parsons.) London, Allen and Unwin, 1930,
and TROELTSCH, Ernst: *The Social Teaching of the Christian Churches.* 2 vols. London, Allen and Unwin, 1931,
as well as FROMM, Erich, op. cit.
2 MANNHEIM, Karl: *Systematic Sociology.* Edited by J. S. Erös and W. A. C. Stewart. London, Routledge and Kegan Paul, 1957. (On the social functions of Competition and Co-operation see Chapters VI and VII.)

CHAPTER XII

1 PLATO: *The Republic.* Translated with an Introduction by A. D. Lindsay. London, Dent, 1935.
2 See COOLEY, C. H.: *Social Organization. A Study in the Larger Mind.* New York, C. Scribner and Sons, 1909,
and COOLEY, C. H.: *Human Nature and the Social Order.* New York, C. Scribner and Sons, 1928.
3 RICHMOND, W. K.: *The Permanent Values in Education.* London, Society for the Promotion of Christian Knowledge, 1920.
4 WATSON, Goodwin: 'A Comparison of the Effects of Lax versus Strict Home Training.' Provincetown, Mass. *Journal of Social Psychology.* Vol. V, No. 4, 1934, pp. 102–105.
5 COOK, L. A.: *Community Backgrounds in Education.* New York, McGraw Hill, 1938. This book has a general relevance to the subject considered in the rest of the Chapter.
6 ISAACS, Susan: *The Children We Teach.* London, University of London Press, 1932,
see further BOWLEY, A. H.: *The Natural Development of the Child: Problems of Family Life.* Edinburgh, E. and S. Livingstone Ltd., 1946,
as well as BÜHLER, Charlotte: *The Child and His Family.* London, Kegan Paul, Trench and Trubner, Ltd., 1940.

CHAPTER XIII

[1] WALLER, W.: *The Sociology of Teaching.* New York, John Wiley & Sons, 1932, p. 297.

[2] See LANE, Homer, T.: *Talks to Parents and Teachers.* New York, Hermitage Press, 1949,

and BAZELEY, E. T.: *Homer Lane and the Little Commonwealth.* London, Allen & Unwin-Heinemann, 1928.

[3] NEILL, A. S.: *That Dreadful School. Hearts not Heads in School. Problem Parents.* All published by Jenkins, London.

[4] HEMMING, James and BALLS, Josephine: *The Child is Right: a Challenge to Parents and Other Adults.* London, Longmans Green, 1947.

[5] See WALLER, op. cit., p. 8.

[6] See FINNEY, Ross L.: *A Sociological Philosophy of Education.* New York, Macmillan Co., 1928, p. 160.

[7] See WALLER, op. cit., p. 9.

CHAPTER XIV

[1] LYND, R. S.: *Knowledge for What?* Princeton, University Press, 1939.

[2] DURKHEIM, Emile: *Suicide: A Study in Sociology.* London, Routledge and Kegan Paul, 1952. Glencoe, Ill., The Free Press, 1951.

[3] For the topics mentioned in this chapter see further:

MANNHEIM, Karl: *Man and Society in an Age of Reconstruction.* London, Kegan Paul, Trench, Trubner & Co., 1940.

MANNHEIM, Karl: *Diagnosis of Our Time.* London, Kegan Paul, Trench, Trubner & Co., 1943.

NOHL, H. and PALLAT, L.: 'Die Soziologischen Grundlagen der Erziehung.' In: *Handbuch der Paedagogik*, Vol. 2, chapter 3. Langensalza, Julius Beltz, 1929.

ROUCEK, J. S. *et al.: Sociological Foundations of Education.* New York, Thomas J. Crowell Co., 1942.

YOUNG, K.: *Social Attitudes.* New York, Henry Holt, 1931.

WARNER, W. L.: 'Formal Education and the Social Structure.' *Journal of Educational Psychology.* New York, May 1936.

WARNER, W. L.: *Environment and Education.* Chicago University Press, 1942. (Supplementary Educ. Monogr. No. 59, pp. 16–28.)

WARNER, W. L. *et al.: Who Shall be Educated? The Challenge of Unequal Opportunities.* London, Routledge and Kegan Paul, 1946.

CHAPTER XV

[1] For these problems see:

WEBER, Max.: *From Max Weber—Essays in Sociology.* Ed. by H. H. Gerth and W. Mills. London, Routledge and Kegan Paul, 1947,

as well as WEBER, Max: 'The Theory of Social and Economic Organization.' Being Part I of *Wirtschaft und Gesellschaft* translated by A. R. Henderson and Talcott Parsons, London, W. Hodge, 1947.

OTHER PUBLICATIONS MENTIONED
PASSIM BY KARL MANNHEIM

ADAMS, Sir John: *Modern Developments of Educational Practice.* London, University of London Press, 1929.
ADAMSON, J. W.: *The Educational Works of John Locke.* London, Longmans, Green & Co., 1912.
AIKIN, W. M.: *The Story of the Eight Year Study.* New York, Harper, 1942.
BAVELAS, A. and LEWIN, K.: 'Training in Democratic Leadership.' *The Journal of Abnormal and Social Psychology* 37. January, 1942, Washington D.C. pp. 115–119.
BRUBACHER, J. S.: *Modern Philosophies of Education,* New York, McGraw Hill Book Co., 1939.
CUBER, F.: 'The Cultural Relativity of Education.' In Roucek, J. S. (Ed.): *Sociological Foundations of Education.* The Thomas Crowell Co., New York, 1942.
FENICHEL, O.: *The Psychoanalytic Theory of Neuroses.* New York, Norton and Co., 1945.
GLASS, Ruth: *The Social Background of a Plan. A Study of Middlesbrough.* London, Routledge and Kegan Paul, 1948.
GREEN, G. H.: *Psychoanalysis in the Classroom.* London, University of London Press, 1932.
HARRIS, P. E.: *Changing Conceptions of School Discipline.* New York, Macmillan Co., 1928.
HEYMANN, K.: *Erziehung als Friedensweg.* Zurich-New York, Europa Verlag, 1945.
JONES, A. J. (with Grinzell, E. D. and Grinstead, W. J.): *Principles of Unit Construction.* New York & London, McGraw Hill Book Co., 1939.
LASKER, Bruno: *Race Attitudes in Children.* New York, H. Holt & Co., 1929.
LODGE, R. C.: *Philosophy of Education.* New York, Harpers, 1934.
MAYO, E.: *The Social Problems of an Industrial Civilization.* London, Routledge and Kegan Paul, 1949.
OTTO, M. C.: *Things and Ideals.* New York, Holts, 1924.
OGBURN, W. F. (ed): *Social Change.* Chicago, University of Chicago Press, 1929.
SZÉKELY, L.: 'Studien zur Psychologie des Denkens: Zur Topologie des Einfalls'. Amsterdam. *Acta Psychologica.* Vol. V. No. 9, 1940 (On creative thinking).
YOUNG, K.: *A Handbook of Social Psychology.* London, Kegan Paul, Trench, Trubner & Co. 1946.

Index

Caste(s), 164
  system, 110
Catholic, 111
Cave, Allegory of (see under
  'Allegory'), 87, 117
Character, 17, 46, 166
  development, 92
  training, 94
Chemistry, 30
Child
  art, 106
  care, 108
  development, 123
Childhood, 92
China, 163
Chinese mandarin, 161
Chivalric tradition, 108
Chivalry, 36-7, 40, 43, 163
Choice, 93, 111
CHRIST (Also see under 'JESUS
  CHRIST'), 120
Christian(-ity), 28, 35, 36, 37, 43,
  44, 120, 160
  doctrine, 87
  gentleman, 22, 43
  group, 45
Church, 36, 37, 92, 110, 119, 148,
  166
  Anglican, 41
  Christian, 44
Cinema, 130, 163
City states, 34
Civil service, 150
CLARKE, F., 9, 19, 48, 167
Class structure, 151
Classes, 46
Classics, 29, 161
Classroom, xv, 105, 119, 134-42
  group, 138
Clergy, 111, 166
Clinics
  Ante-natal, 131
  Child guidance, 80
  Child welfare, 131
  Post-natal, 131
Closure, 60
Cognition, 61
Cognitive capital, 140

Collective monologue, 90
Collectivist, 48
Colleges of Further Education, 131
Common effort, 112
Common sense, 164
Communication, 31
Communist party, 39
Community, 19, 162
Compensation(s), 78, 110
Competition, xiv, 46, 82, 94, 103,
  106, 109, 111, 137, 145
Composition, 81
Compulsion, xiv, 92
Compulsory attendance, 138
COMTE, A., 119
Concentration, 103
Conditioned
  reflex, 56
  response, 67, 68
Conditioning, xiv, 67, 100, 145
  Deconditioning, 58, 59
  Infantile, xiii, 49
  Social, 53-64
Confidence, 102
Conflict(s), 45, 81, 103, 108, 123,
  145, 146, 151
Conformity, xv, 30, 42, 111
CONFUCIUS, 163
Conscience, xiii, 88, 96, 111
Conscious mind, 27
Containment, 46
Control, 148
COOK, L. A., 124, 173
COOLEY, C. H., 89, 119, 121, 172, 173
Co-operation, 45, 46, 94, 137, 145
Co-operative-to-school homes, 127-8
Courage, 163
Courtesy, 37
Crafts, 30
Creativeness, xiv, xv, 105, 111
Creator, 98
Criminology, 4
Crisis, 147
Crusades, 43
Cue, 56, 70, 71
Cultural
  conservation, 101
  lag, 30

Moral personality, 97
  philosophy, 118
  problems, 145
  qualities, 95
  standards, 123
MORENO, J. L., xiv, 93, 96, 98, 101,
  105, 172, 173
MORRIS, W., 165
Motivation(s), 62, 65, 66, 67, 93, 104
Motives, 96
Music, 30, 34, 100, 102, 172, 173
  as an art form, 101

Nation, 47
National characteristics, 71
Nationalism, 46, 146
'Natural' leader, 139
Nazi(s), 6, 8, 146
Neighbourhood, 119
NEILL, A. S., 140, 174
New Education Fellowship, 29
NIEBUHR, R., 121
Nobility, 39
Normality, 77
Norms, 40, 112, 147
NUNN, P., 47, 48, 169
NYBERG, P., viii

Obedience, 112
Old Testament, 35
Organ defect, 78
  inferiority, 77
Originator, 99
Our Town, 6
OWEN, R., 29

PAINTER, F. V. N., 167
Painting, 105
Palestine, xii
Parent(s), 78, 94, 102, 123, 124
  child relationship, 107
  teachers' associations, 129
Parliament, 150
Passivity, 81, 82
PAVLOV, J. P., 56, 58, 170
Pedagogy, 3
Perception(s), 67, 92

Perfect systems, 29
Person, 64
Personal leadership, 139
Personality, xii, xiv, 28, 32, 34, 44,
  47, 49, 50, 63, 64, 78, 79, 83,
  87-99, 103, 139, 145, 161, 166
  inventory, 105
  structure, 107, 124, 128
  theory, 78
Philosopher, 112
Philosopher-kings, 87
Philosophy, 146
  Political and moral, 150
Physical development, 102
Physics, 30
PIAGET, J., 90, 91, 172
Piety, 163
Planning, 165
  for freedom, 44
PLATO (Platonic), 34, 87, 117, 172,
  173
Play, 101
Play group(s), 92, 119, 148
Police, 150
Politics, 31, 46, 113, 146
Political
  opportunism, 146
  parties, 150
Position of women, 148
Power, 136, 148, 150
Pragmatism, 146
Praise, 81
Prefects, 30
Prestige, 139, 148
Press, 163
Priests, 111
Primary
  group(s), 117, 145
  sources, 166
Problem-solving, 60
Profession(s), 131, 148
Professional standards, 152
Progressive Movement, 29
Projection, 62
Propaganda, 144
Property rights, 46
Protestantism, 38, 110, 111
'Pseudo-conversation,' 90

Secondary stage, 129
Security, 123
Selection, 137, 166
  for secondary education, 129, 137
Self, xii, xiv, 49, 70, 71, 88, 93, 96,
  97, 99, 106, 107, 161
  'I', xiv, 93, 96, 97
  'me', xiv, 93, 96
  -assertive, 61, 94
  -assertiveness, 109
  -assertion, 62, 69
  -esteem, 93
  -control, 69, 163, 164
  -expression, 100
  -identification, 97
  -realization, 29
  Act, 98
  Content, 98
  Emergence of the, 88
Selfhood, 88, 89, 92
Self-regarding
  attitude, 93
  sentiments, 80
Sense experience, 68
Sentiments, 162
Sex, 79
Sexual, 27
  impetus, 58
Sexuality, 78
Shyness, 56, 77
Simplicity, 34
Skill, 45
SKINNER, C. E., 64, 99, 171
Sleep, 61
SMITH, A., 46
Social
  conformity, 163
  development, 91
  disorganization, 146
  distinction, 161
  forces, 145
  geographers, 119
  groups, 148
  institutions, 121, 147
  justice, 120
  maturity, 92
  order, 151
  psychologist(s), xiii

Social
  psychology, xv, 140, 142
  sciences, 31
  self, 94
  selection, 152, 164
  services, 23-4, 121
  studies, 31
Socialization, 62
Socialism(-ists), 165
Society, 19, 20, 33, 38, 43, 47, 48,
  49, 50, 54, 94, 106, 107, 109, 110,
  111, 119, 120, 121, 123, 145, 146,
  147, 148, 149, 153, 160, 164
  Competitive, 133, 137
  Educative, 15, 20, 136
  Medieval, 164
  Western, 133
Societies, 32, 149
Sociologist, 148
Sociology, 9, 10, 11, 31
  of culture, x
  of knowledge, x
  of teaching, 153-54
Socio-drama (see also under
  'Drama', 'Psycho-drama'), 105
Sociometric tests, 105
SOCRATES, 34, 118
Soldier, 34
Soul, 87
Sparta, 34, 35
Speech
  Egocentric, 90
  Socialized, 90
Spelling, 80, 81
SPENCER, H., 119
Spontaneity, xiv, 98, 100, 102, 105,
  111
  theory, 104
Spontaneous
  achievement, 103
  action, 102
  creation, 101
  energy, 102, 103
  impulses, 104
  relationships, 136
Sport, 95
Stakhanovite worker, 164
Standard, 102, 103, 148